*The Survival Guide for Highly Sensitive People
to Empath Healing:
How to Develop Your Gift & Spirituality
to Become an Awakened Empath and Mystic*

Judith Brown

Table of Contents

PART ONE: UNDERSTANDING EMPATHS 7

CHAPTER ONE: WHAT EMPATHS ARE 8

EMPATHY AND EMPATH 11
THE SCIENCE BEHIND EMPATH 13
UNDERSTANDING YOUR ENERGY 17

CHAPTER TWO: EMPATH AND ITS FORMS 23

TYPES OF EMPATH 26
EMPATH AND SPIRITUALITY 31

CHAPTER THREE: THE EMPATH'S TRAITS 35

THE HABITS OF EMPATHS 40

PART TWO: LIVING YOUR EMPATH'S STATUS 45

CHAPTER FOUR: EMPATHS AND RELATIONSHIP 46

BALANCING YOUR GIFT AS AN EMPATH AND YOUR RELATIONSHIP 51
HOW TO DEAL WITH AN EMPATH IN A RELATIONSHIP 54

CHAPTER FIVE: EMPATH AND WORK 59

HOW EMPATHS REACT TO THEIR WORK ENVIRONMENT 60
DEALING WITH EMPATH AT WORK 67

CHAPTER SIX: UTILIZING YOUR SPIRITUAL GIFTS RIGHTLY	**71**
HOW TO UTILIZE YOUR GIFTS RIGHTLY	75
PART THREE: PROTECTING YOURSELF AND GIFT	**81**
CHAPTER SEVEN: UNDERSTANDING NEGATIVE ENERGIES	**82**
TYPES OF NEGATIVE ENERGY	84
EMPATHS AND DEPRESSION	88
EMPATHS AND INSOMNIA/FATIGUE	91
CHAPTER EIGHT: TECHNIQUES TO DEAL WITH NEGATIVE ENERGIES	**94**
THE SHIELDING TECHNIQUE	95
THE GROUNDING TECHNIQUE	99
THE CLEARING TECHNIQUE	103
CHAPTER NINE: DEALING WITH ADDICTIONS	**108**
HOW TO KNOW IF YOU'RE ADDICTED	111
HOW TO DEAL WITH YOUR ADDICTIONS	113
CONCLUSION	**117**

INTRODUCTION

Twenty percent of the world population is made of highly sensitive people. If you are reading this book, you are probably one of them. The highly sensitive people in our world are angels in human form. They give to us of their abundance. They are healers who take up the emotions of others. I wonder what our world would look like without these people. There would be thousands of emotionally drained humans plying the nooks and crannies of our world. The highly sensitive people are those next to the therapy that the world needs. However, many people do not know much about these gems. More alarming is the fact that most of these creatures do not know much about themselves. They carry unique power and ability that distinguish them from other human beings around them.

Many people only see empaths as healers. They fail to see the pains they also go through. Taking up other people's emotions is more burdensome than anyone can think. It is a load that is added to an already existing load. Every Empath stands at the risk of experiencing energy drainage from the overload of emotions that they are exposed to. There is a risk of negative energy hovering around them. All these often result in addictions when they are not adequately dealt with. More challenges are present before empaths. There are relationship challenges, and the work environment challenges as well. Although we all face challenges that are similar to these challenges, empaths experience is quite different and requires a different approach.

In this book, you will be guided on how to deal with the listed problems that you are likely to face as an empath. I have critically examined how you can protect your energy from the influence of bad energy, how you can protect yourself from energy drainage, and how you can deal with addictions. Also, this book will guide you into how you can be effective in your relationships as an empath, and it will aid others who are not empaths to have an ideal understanding of how to relate with you. It will guide you on how best you can perform at your workplace and enjoy your gift. This book is the solution and answer to many problems you are likely to face as an empath and any questions you have on the realities of being an empath. OPEN THE FIRST PAGE OF THIS BOOK AND BEGIN THE JOURNEY THAT WILL GUIDE YOU INTO BEING A BETTER EMPATH OR CREATING A BETTER RELATIONSHIP WITH EMPATHS IF YOU ARE NOT ONE.

PART ONE

UNDERSTANDING EMPATHS

CHAPTER ONE

WHAT EMPATHS ARE

In our world today, we have many people who show specific super ordinary abilities. These people are quite difficult to lie to in whatever instance you may think. Can you imagine having a friend who is so emotional and sensitive to you? He or she sometimes may end up feeling your pain and happiness. How do you plan to react to such a friend?

On the other hand, let me change the direction of the questions. Have you ever been told of your oversensitivity? Do you observe you are frequently too emotional? Perhaps you have a sense of anxiety when you are among the crowd. Do you often feel drained when you are around certain people? Besides, has it ever occurred to you that when your friends share a unique experience, you find yourself feeling the same way they felt? A yes to these questions is a reflection that you probably belong to a group of special people in our world today – the Empaths. In the subsequent chapters of this book, I will be taking you through the realities of these people, and I will give you an in-depth understanding on how to deal with them and at the same time how you (If you are an empathy) can utilize your power to achieve a better self.

WHAT IS EMPATH?

Empaths are people with a high level of sensitivity to what happens around them. These people can know the thoughts and emotions of others around them. Psychologists are interested in the topic, and they relate it to empathy. The term Empath also functions in spiritual space. When it is used in the spiritual space, an Empath is an individual with special and psychic abilities to gain access to others' emotions and energies. The ability of empaths sometimes is voluntary and involuntary. Involuntary occurs to people who are born naturally with the ability to feel others' emotions and thoughts. Empaths are often hypersensitive with a high level of compassion, understanding, and consideration toward others. Their ability makes them receive the pain and emotions of others, but they do not have a clear understanding of how it happens. Empaths are difficult to hide your feelings from; they will always have a deep insight into your feelings and relationship with you based on your feeling. The empath's ability is not constrained by time or distance. Regardless of the distance, an empath can feel the emotions of others.

Empaths play significant roles in our environment. They are highly creative and productive. Most Empaths are bards in motion. Certain natural talents reside in them. Among them, we often have writers, artists, musicians, actors. They are well-grounded with imagination and creativity. Often, they are broad-minded, and they accept all forms of culture without any biases. Empaths are not restricted to a particular culture or territory. They are everywhere. In all spheres of life across the globe, you will likely find Empaths. The challenge may be to recognize them; nonetheless, they are everywhere. You should not be surprised that you may have an Empath in your family. Perhaps your wife, husband, first son, or last child is an Empath. If you have not noticed the kind of personality your family members have, and you have been wondering about the science and reason behind their behavior, you will get the answer to the question you seek in this book. Regardless of gender and color, Empaths are everywhere. They are experts at listening to others, problem solvers, philosophers in their thinking and studies. They are often highly optimistic; for every problem, they believe there will surely be an answer. The basic attribute of every empath is *empathy.*

EMPATHY AND EMPATH

Empathy is the feeling of care about other people. Empathy occurs when we put ourselves in the situation of others to understand what they are going through. With empathy, it will be easier for anyone to be in tune with the feelings of the other persons around him or her. All humans have the capacity to empathize. At times, empathy relies on your experience to relate to the emotions of the other person. For instance, if your friend loses a family member, you will be able to understand his or her feelings by relating the episode with your loss. At one time or another, we all have someone dear to us that we end up losing. The experience will help us to relate with others later when they find themselves in the same situation. Empathy gives you the capacity to share in the other person's experience. Empathy is all about feeling the other person's emotions. Empathy does not give you the ability to share in the other person's pain.

Empath, on the other hand, takes the function of empathy a little further. Empaths take up other peoples' experience intuitively without relying on any experience or external cues. An empath is so strong that it can even relate to other creatures, such as animals, plants, minerals, and rocks, which the empath does not share any nature with. Although all empaths have empathy, empathy is not totally the same as being an empath. While empathy is at the surface, being an empath goes deeper into the core emotions of the subjects involved.

The primary difference between empathy and being an empath lies in the role of experience and external cues that a person utilizes while empathizing. The feeling of empathy often requires some triggers, which may include a phone call or the saddened face of the person you want to empathize with. Empaths do not require any of these. Even when a person tries to hide his or her feelings, empaths are so sensitive that they will access the issue and speak on it. Empaths only need to observe someone else's energy, consciously and unconsciously, to understand his or her emotions. The physical meeting is needless to gain access. Empaths work like medium, and they can heal every pain of the people around them. People have empath as a gift.

Nonetheless, empathy has its usefulness. It creates bonding and strengthens relationships. Through empathy, we can create intimacy, trust, compassion, reference, and possibly belonging. All empaths have the empathy spirit in them, but not everyone who empathizes is an empath.

THE SCIENCE BEHIND EMPATH

The functionality of empaths has influenced psychologists and neuroscientists to carry out studies on how the personality works. There is an opinion that empathy is perhaps the therapy we need in this world to cure us all of our ailments. Since empaths are high on the empathic spectrum, and they feel the feelings and pains of others, they tend to be compassionate and considerate. Just imagine having your boss as an Empath. Your work stress will reduce unless he or she is a psychopath. He or she is expected to have access to your emotions and understand the best time to allocate certain functions to you. Our world will change if we all have one or two empaths in our lives. The ability to feel others' pain and emotions can overwhelm the Empaths and affect their lives. They need to understand the strategies they need to overcome the challenges that follow their ability. There have been studies on the abilities of empaths and empathy. These studies show how empaths can gain access to others' emotions and thoughts. The scientific studies gave five explanations on how empaths function.

- **The Mirror Neuron System**

Under this explanation, the researchers identified a specific group of cells in the human brain that helps to form compassion. These cells are responsible for peoples' ability to project others' emotions, to partake of their fear, pains, or happiness. The hypersensitive nature of Empaths relies on the hyper-responsive mirror neurons in them. External events often trigger these neurons. When your partner is hurt, in the labor room, or probably feeling stressed, you will feel it alongside him or her. The cry of your baby will grip your heart and make you feel sad also. If your friend loses his job or he or she experiences an accident, you will feel the pain too and be attached. This neuron is lacking in narcissists, sociopaths, and psychopaths, and this is why they have empathy deficiency. They do not show empathy as others do. Rather than having an active mirror neuron system, they possess an under-active mirror neuron system that does not make them show compassion. These people do not show love; they are often dangerous, and usually, they try to hurt others.

- **Electromagnetic Fields Explanation**

The scientists further probe into how empathy and empaths work; they identify specific electromagnetic fields that both the human brain and heart generate. These electromagnetic fields help to transmit information concerning the emotion, feelings, pains, and thoughts of the other people. The electromagnetic fields heighten the sensitivity of the Empaths and make them aware of the information it transmits, which may overwhelm the empaths. Besides, empaths are often aware of the changes in the earth and sun, and they usually give strong physical and emotional responses to those changes. What happens to the earth, the sun affects the state of mind of empaths, and frequently, they know about it. Similarly, when there are changes in the electromagnetic fields of the earth and sun, empaths give strong physical and emotional responses. They are aware of the effects of the changes on our state of mind and energy.

- **The Phenomenon of Emotional Contagion**

The phenomenon of emotional contagion helps to enhance our comprehension of how the empaths function. Aside from being an empath, studies have revealed that, naturally, many people pick up the feelings and pains of the people that surround them. A practical example is an infant in a hospital. If an infant begins to cry in the ward, it will spark up a wave of crying among other infants in the ward. If a person is experiencing stress and anxiety in the workplace, if it is not curtailed in time, it can spread to other workers. It is not uncommon for people to contact other peoples' feelings in groups. This explanation shows that emotions are contagious, and this is one reason empaths gain access to other people's emotions and thoughts. This ability to synchronize our moods with other people can be an excellent tool for creating a balanced relationship. If you are an empath, this explanation is showing a critical way forward to avoid bad energy, which is for you to surround yourself with positive people and avoid negative ones to avoid negative influence on you. Later in this book, I will take you through the steps to take to overcome the challenges that come with emotional contagion.

- **High Dopamine Sensitivity**

The studies present a fourth explanation of how empaths and empathy work the way they do. This explanation involves dopamine, which is a neurotransmitter that helps to increase the activity of neurons. It is also responsible for the responses we have to please. According to the studies, introverted empaths are prone to a higher rate of sensitivity to dopamine than their extroverts counterparts do. The introverted empaths need less dopamine to feel happy or pleasure. They often enjoy aloneness, reading, and meditation with less or no stimulation from others. However, the extroverts among the empaths enjoy the dopamine rush they get from external stimulations, such as the gathering of people or events. They often have difficulty enjoying the dopamine rush, as it is never enough for them and are always in need of more of it; hence, they socialize and go for parties to have the dopamine rush. The extrovert empaths are not shy and often rely on external stimulation.

- **The Synesthesia Explanation**

The last explanation of the dimensions in the working of an empath's brain is on synesthesia. It is also known as the "mirror-touch synesthesia." It involves two distinct senses of the human brain that are paired in a neurological state. How this happens is that you will see colors while you listen to music, or you perhaps feel like tasting words. The mirror-touch synesthesia makes you feel the emotions and sensations of others as if all is happening in your body. This gives the overall explanation as to why empaths take on others' feelings and emotions as their own. It often overwhelms the empaths because, by taking on others' emotions and stress, they have double loads on their heads. Aside from their emotions, they need to take on other peoples' emotions.

Empathy is the most valuable quality humans possess. It helps us to establish healthy relationships and live in peace with others. Empathy prevents us from being sentimental and exposes us to discernment to understand the other person and their challenges. We see people in light of ourselves, and we make them feel good, which in turn affects the way they also perceive and respect us. Your tolerance rate will increase as much as you can empathize with the other person, and this will prevent you from getting unnecessarily angry.

UNDERSTANDING YOUR ENERGY

The human body is made of five layers of energy. The first layer is your body. Your body has weight, volume, and shape. It can be touched, seen, and felt. The other four layers surround the physical body; however, they are not easy to see. We call these other four layers a person's aura. These five layers of energy make up the human energy field. The layers store our psychological, physical, spiritual, and emotional characteristics. It is possible to have balanced energy or imbalanced energy; this is why it is often advisable in medicine that medical care should go beyond the physical body, and attention should be paid to the other characteristics.

The aura is the auric field or radiance of a person. An electromagnetic field surrounds the being of an individual. A particular set of people, such as energy medical practitioners, have access to see the movement of the aura. The aura is like a magnet that picks up energies floating around us. You need to cleanse your energy from time to time to prevent it from negative energies and some alien vibrations that may impede it. Auras in the form of color and light often revolve around our physical bodies. Some people can see these auras around us as much as they can see any part of our body. This possibility is a confirmation that we are spiritual beings, while our physical bodies are just secondary to our real nature. Our aura is susceptible to attracting bad energies if we do not curb it as soon as possible. The human aura can experience stress, the loss of luminosity, and fragmentation. You can apply the physical and mental methods to cleanse your aura.

Mental Cleansing: The mental cleansing involves you visualizing the negative energies and ridding it off psychologically. It places the onus on you to eradicate your mind of negative energies that may deter you. To achieve mental cleansing, you need to take the following steps:

- You are required to sit in a quiet place where there are no distractions and sit in a relaxed manner for about 15 minutes.
- Practice breathing exercises and remain conscious so you can be aware of how you inhale and exhale.
- You can switch to meditation after the breathing exercise.
- Once you are relaxed, create white light in your mind and surround yourself with it. Permit it to flow through you, starting from the tips of your toes to the top of your head and try to visualize it moving up and down your back.

Combing Your Aura: It is a visualization exercise. You need to combine the visualization with physical activity. It involves you washing your hands thoroughly, and you will spread your fingers into a comb and comb the space that surrounds your body. You should start from your head and move downward to the toes. Then, clean your hands with water to let all combed up energies wash away.

Use Water for Cleansing: Water has powerful properties to help wash away negative energies from you. Cleansing with water is possible either physically or by visualizing it. You make sure that you allow water to flow over every part of your body, including your head, face, shoulder, arm, torso, legs, and finally, to your feet. Watch the water flow away and give yourself a relief breathe and imagine all negative energy flowing away from your mind alongside the water. To make the cleansing by water effective, you can add salt to the water. Salt contains essential healing properties that heal the human body. You may also swim in salt. Also, rainwater is a good method you can adopt to cleanse your body. Walk outside in the rain and lookup. Allow the water coming from above to cleanse you from head to your feet.

Use Feather Whisk: Feather whisk is a physical object you can use to help clean your aura of bad energies. Your choice of a feather should be that of an Owl or Turkey. Use the feather to make a sweeping motion through the space that surrounds your body. Start the sweep from your feet and sweep it upward. You should request the help of someone to help you sweep certain parts of your body that you do not have access to, such as your back.

Utilize the Smudge Ritual: The smudging ritual involves you using smoke from dried white sage or other herbs to clean your aura. It is common in America. You need to light the edge of a smudge stick and wait until it releases flame. The stick will keep producing smoke as it burns, and you need to encircle it around yourself. Make it go round your body from your feet and move up. The smoke will cleanse your energy as you move it around you. Moving it around, you will give it access to your energy. You can use many herbs for this purpose. Some of the herbs are lavender, sweetgrass, and sage.

You must protect your aura from negative energies. Negative energies put you down and limit your progress in creativity and productivity. One way to protect your aura is to fill yourself with the right set of people – the positive-minded ones. Also, make yourself see the best of everything you encounter from time to time and don't look at the evil part of life. Always see the bright side of everything you experience.

IDENTIFYING YOUR ENERGY FIELDS

Apart from the physical energy field, it takes a special ability to see the four other energy fields. The clairvoyant ability is often required to see these four energy fields. Clairvoyance is the ability to see hidden things. The other four energy fields sometimes look different when compared with others. Also, some people are trained to identify these layers. They can sense a person's aura just by touching, scents, or even sound. The layers are energies that have a pulse that can be measured. The five physical layers of human energy are below.

1. **Physical Energy:** The physical energy is the layer we all perceive to be ourselves. The physical energy consists of flesh, bone, skin, organs, and blood. It is the physical energy that everyone can see, and it has similar strength as the ones we cannot see.
2. **Etheric Energy:** It is from the word *ether,* which is a layer of our energy body. It is located approximately one and a half inches away from the physical body. Energy practitioners have stated that it is like a spider web; it is sticky and stretchy in away. It is either gray or gray-blue. The practitioners have considered the etheric as the blueprint or holograph of the physical body.
3. **The Emotional Energy:** The emotional energy is located at the center of the five layers. It contains human feelings and fears. It is volatile, especially when an individual is experiencing either a high or a low emotion.
4. **Mental Energy:** It is the fourth layer. This is the seat of ideas and values. The belief system of every human being is stored in mental energy. The mental energy helps to process human thoughts, sieve them, sort them, and possibly assimilate them.

All human opinions and beliefs stem from mental energy. Whatever we stand for in the real world is a function of the thoughts we have processed in our mental energy.
5. **The Spiritual Energy:** This layer takes our consciousness and higher awareness into custody. It often relates us to our past lives and experiences, and at the same time, it relates us to universal consciousness.

CHAPTER TWO:

EMPATH AND ITS FORMS

I have mentioned earlier that empaths are highly sensitive personalities. They have varying egress of emotional intelligence in them, and this gives them the ability to understand others at every point beyond our expectations. Usually, they tend to be shy and quiet among people; however, they have a rich and complex inner life that they try to keep from the world. Their understanding of others makes them listen more to others than they speak. You can consider them excellent communicators. Though all empaths have similar attributes in terms of their sensitivity, they are different in other respects. I will look into the three general categorizations of empaths and the different types of empathy.

Categorization of Empath

There are different types of Empaths in our world; however, these forms can be categorized under three broad forms. These categorizations will show the general attitudes and attributes of Empaths across different types. In the categorization, I will be highlighting the distinguishing central attribute of each category of Empath. The three forms are:

- **The Cognitive Empaths**

This category of Empath is distinguished by their high emotional intelligence. They show significant strength in understanding other people's behavior. They have the capacity and understanding of how they can separate themselves from other behavior. They look at things differently, considering different perspectives. They are not limited in their view and scope. They have an understanding of why someone acts in a particular manner, and they often understand the reason behind every act. Their cognition is often geared toward being considerate about others based on their understanding.

- **The Affective Empaths**

Just like the cognitive empaths, affective empaths also possess the ability to understand other intelligence emotionally and others' ways of thinking. They, however, added to the ability of the cognitive is their ability to absorb others' emotions and experience. This set of Empath is prone to negative energy. The Empaths are too attached to others. When you have a relationship with them, you are in close range with their emotions, and they have access to your burdens. Their talents make it difficult and overwhelming for them to stay in a large group. They usually avoid the crowd. At the same time, they try to get away from intimate relationships because they are too affectionate, and their affection can be a source of trouble, as they will likely forgo their challenges for the challenges of the other person. Others' needs often come before their needs.

- **The Compassionate Empaths**

The feeling of others usually moves this category of Empath, and the emotional attachment often leads them to take action. The successes of how they relate to others depend on how well they are able to utilize their abilities. If they utilize their empathy rightly, they proffer solutions to people's challenges and issues. However, they can take their empathy too far and, as such, confuse the other people's feelings and theirs.

All these categories of Empaths can be balanced. Empathy can take over a person's mind easily; as a result, it is essential for an empath to make setting healthy boundaries a practice. These healthy boundaries will help the Empath deal with certain deficiencies and negative energies that may revolve around him or her. In a later chapter, I will take you through how you can deal with negative energies as an Empath.

TYPES OF EMPATH

With the understanding of the categorization of empaths, you need to know the type of Empath that you are. These types are divided based on their characteristics and their object of affections. When you have an understanding of the type of Empath you belong, it will be easier for you to make the most of your gift, while you take care of yourself. There are seven basic types of empaths, and these differences lie in the gaps in their empathetic abilities.

1. **The Emotional Empath**

This is one of the commonest empaths you can find around. It is a form of affective Empath. The emotional Empath finds it easy to pick the emotions and feelings of people around him or her. They do not stop at picking it up but also feeling the same emotions as if they belong to them. Their emotional body tries to take on the emotions of others, and they express it as much as the other person does; an emotional empath will be sad if he or she is with a person experiencing sadness. Their emotional strength often depends on others'feelings, and they are easily drawn to happiness or sadness depending on the kind of people and events that surround them at every point in time. The consequence of this sharing of emotions prevents emotional Empaths from helping other people who need their help. Before they can offer a hand of help, they are already drained by the feeling of sadness they share with the other person around them. Unless an emotional empath learns to differentiate between his or her emotions and that the others, it will be difficult for the Empath to help others with their abilities.

2. **The Medical/Physical Empath**

These empaths are empowered to take the energies of other people's bodies. They, by intuition, know the method that ails other people, and they often act as healers. They often carry out the healing skills either as a medical practitioner or in an alternative means. They often have a feeling of awareness in their bodies when they are treating others, and they can see "blockage" in someone's energy field, which they sense requires urgent treatment. A medical empath can pick the symptoms of sickness from the other person and feel it in his or her body. When a physical empath takes the symptoms of others, it often hampers the health of the Empath. The medical Empath with serious illnesses, such as fibromyalgia or autoimmune, might find those diseases helpful. The diseases will help to strengthen their energetic fields, so they will have the ability to turn their abilities off when it is necessary. Also, the Empath needs to take certain training in healing. The training will help to deal with the negative impacts of the medical empath traits they possess.

3. **Geomantic Empath**

This is also environmental or places Empath. The environmental empaths are often fine-tuned to the physical landscape of their environment. How do you know you are an environmental empath? You know this if you find out that a certain area or place makes you feel uncomfortable, while a certain environment makes you feel happy without any reason whatsoever. There will be a deep connection between you and a particular place. Some geomantic empaths are drawn to physical objects in a place, such as a sacred stone, groves, or a church. The place empaths often place their emotions on the history they pick up about a certain place. They are sensitive to the narrative that follows a particular place establishment or development. If the stories present past of brutality or enslavement, the environmental Empath will feel sad. The previous events in a specific location may arouse joy or fear in the Empath. They usually feel horrific when trees are cut and landscapes undergo destruction.

Environmental empaths require nature to empower themselves. Engaging in environmental projects is also a good way to enable them. The Geomantic empaths need to make their everyday harmonious and beautiful as much as possible. You will get places from plants and natural scents. Whatever is natural often goes well for the environmental empaths. You can go for natural linen in clothing and furniture.

4. **The Plant or Flora Empath**

This type of Empath has a special ability. Just like the botanist, the plant empath has a full understanding of a plant. They have the right information on the right place to arrange a plan for a garden at every point in time; you will usually find many plant empaths working in gardens, parks, or wild landscapes, where they can put their skills and abilities to use. Some of the empaths get their guidance from trees and plants by hearing them speak directly through their minds. The plant empath can communicate with plants. This kind of Empath establishes relationships with plants rather than humans, and all their musing is centered on the plants around them. The plant empaths require many contacts with plants and trees. If you are a plant empath, you can strengthen your bond with plants by attuning yourself more intimately to it; sit quietly under or beside a special tree or plant.

5. **The Animal or Fauna Empath**

Animals serve as connections to many empaths. Just like the plant empaths, an animal empath will gain strength by staying close to animals. There will be a certain level of love that exists in the empath individual. Empaths care for animals often, and they understand the needs of the animal. They can carry out telepathic communication with an animal. To be considered an animal empath, you perhaps have spent more time with animals. By studying the biology or psychology of animals, you will be able to refine your abilities. The animal empath functions optimally as an animal doctor. The profession goes hand in hand with their talents. It will be easier for them to treat and heal animals because they have the inherent potentials to identify when an animal needs treatment, and with the knowledge of animal medicine, it will become easier for them to treat them accordingly.

6. **The Intuitive or Claircognizant Empath**

The intuitive empaths work like a hotspot. Whenever they are within the range of others, they will pick up their emotions and feelings. They gather information about others ordinarily by staying close to them. With a glance, the claircognizant empaths have loads of information about the person. They are difficult to lie to because they have access to your thoughts and intentions. The intuitive empaths look like super-ordinary humans. The empaths can read other energy easily. This type of Empath requires the right set of people to be around them. Make sure the people you surround yourself with are those that are in alignment with you. At the same time, you need to strengthen your energetic field so that you will not be bombarded constantly with other people's thoughts and emotions.

7. **The Medium Empath**

The medium empaths act as a medium. They feel the emotions of spirits that cross over. Unlike an ordinary medium who can see and communicate with spirit only, a medium empath can sense the emotion of the spirit, and the emotions will draw him or her. The Empath can hear and see the spirit sometimes and understand how the spirit feels.

One thing that connects all types of Empaths is their emotional abilities. An empath will have feelings toward plants, animals, the environment, or humans. In every instance, emotion has a crucial role to play. It is not easy to be an empath. It is often confusing, disorientating, and exhausting. However, with the understanding of the type of an empath that you are, you will be able to utilize the gift effectively.

EMPATH AND SPIRITUALITY

Empaths are connected to spirituality. The form of Empath that has a connection with spirituality is the medium Empath, also called the spiritual Empath. Empaths have a direct connection to the spiritual realm. They feel connected to the spirit realm and understand the feelings of the spirits. More than communicating with the spirit realm as a medium, there is a stronger bond between empaths and spirituality. This connection leads to a powerful spiritual reawakening. One difficult experience you can have is knowing when your emotions will be calm, balanced, and collected. Sometimes, it sounds difficult that you can have a clear and balanced state; however, it is possible. It will demand a lot from you. When you want to achieve spiritual awakening, your empathic abilities will be of help. You may feel like your empathic qualities are burdensome; know that it is the process for spiritual awakening. During spiritual awakening, your emotions and empathy will become highly sensitive. You will experience some feelings that show the connection between your empath skills and the process of spiritual awakening. These feelings serve as the signs and symptoms of an empath's powerful spiritual awakening.

- You will have the feeling that something is changing in you or has changed in you. You will not be able to explain it, but you will feel the difference in yourself. You will see the new person you are as different from the old person you used to be. The world, to you, will take on new colors and tastes.
- You will become aware of your past negative habits. The past thinking patterns that you wish to change will come to you. The actions you took earlier that you no longer want to take.

All of these will become clear to you. You will see yourself as ready for a change and not ready to go back.
- You will not feel good with your old company anymore. You will feel the need to change your past entourage and be alone or place yourself among new people who are in alignment with who you are and what you stand for. The need to change the people around you lies in the requirement of evolving spiritually. Spiritual awakening is often a painful and demanding process. Not everyone around you will develop with you at the same rate. Some of the people will try to pull you down or slow your pace. You will need to identify those who will energize you and empower you to press forward.
- The empathic traits in you will make you allergic to whatever is superficial and unreal. You will deal with authentic things, people, and plans.
- Spiritual awakening is usually followed by the feeling of despair at the sickness of the world. You will begin to feel sad and have deep despair toward the situation of the world around you. As you become more aware of the issues in the world, your sadness will increase toward the suffering of the world.
- At this point, the feeling of sadness you have will lead you to think of the best means to make the world better. The spiritual awakening you get with your empathic abilities will not make you consider yourself only. You always want to do something for the world, probably by identifying a way to help the world improve. Your compassion for others will deepen daily. The result of this is that you will feel happy whenever you are able to help someone. There will be a sense of fulfillment each time you can alleviate someone's problem.

- At the last feeling, you want to acquire meaning for your life also. Since you have lost interest in the previous things you were into, now you need to find meaning for your life to avoid boredom. To achieve the meaning you want for your life, you need to create a purpose for your life and find a job you can do. The jobs that will come to your mind will be those that will help the world. You will avoid depression by avoiding boredom.

CHAPTER THREE

THE EMPATH'S TRAITS

Every creature has specific traits that distinguish it from others. Dogs bark, observe, respect, and protect their owner's properties. The lion is a king in the jungle; it rules over the glade and earns the respect of those around it. Humans have the general traits that make us consider them as human. However, the disparities that exist among humans that differentiate them from one another is determined by certain varying traits that they exhibit. Empaths are a set of people who have certain characteristics that differentiate them from other people. They are hypersensitive, and this makes them attract the attention of others. You may be an empath and perhaps not fully aware. At the end of this chapter, you will have a full glimpse of your realities and know the activities you need to note if you are to identify whether you are an empath or not. I will be taking you through twelve characteristics of empaths that you need to watch out for whenever you need to identify an empath.

The hallmark of an Empath is your ability to feel and take in others' emotions as a result of high sensitivity. An empath filters the world through his or her intuition with difficulty in understanding his or her feelings.

#Trait 1 – High Sensitivity

Empaths are the gift of God to humanity in terms of their ability to understand the feelings of others. They are good listeners, open, and naturally giving. They are sensitive to the needs of others and understand what should be done at every point in time in their relationship with others. There is an increased sensitivity of their central nervous systems; they have deeper cognitive processing of physical, social, and emotional stimuli. Their understanding of what others need and request empowers them to serve a therapeutic role in healing and providing the help that the people around them need. They can be hurt, on the other hand. They often need to toughen up.

#Trait 2 – Absorbing Emotions

Just as a foam in water sucks in as much as possible, empaths are prone to other people's emotions. They usually take on other people's moods – good or bad, and feel it, as they would have. When an empath moves close to a person, the Empath will feel the pains and joy of the person the same way the person would experience it and even sometimes to the extreme. This trait either helps or hampers them. When they are people with negative thoughts, they pick it up while it weighs them down; however, when they are with positive people, they are elevated, and they experience joy and flourish.

#Trait 3 – Introversive

Empaths are introverts. They usually enjoy staying alone and being free from the crowd. When they are amidst the crowd, they feel overwhelmed, and this often raises their empathy. You can imagine being placed in a room where five different stereos are playing different songs. There will be noise rather than music. The single euphonious beats of each record will become a conflux of cacophonous noise. Empaths feel similarly when they are among the crowd. Having many emotions surrounding them increases their empath functionality, and they are lost among many emotions. Empaths prefer one-to-one interaction with others. They would rather with a small group of people. In the case of an extrovert who is also an empath, he or she would prefer spending less time with a crowd or at a party.

#Trait 4 – Intuition

Empaths live, basically, on their intuition rather than conscious knowledge. Intuition involves understanding a phenomenon through instinct without necessarily thinking consciously. It is an unconscious knowing that often reveals certain information to a person. Empaths form their opinion about people and the world based on their gut and intuition. Through their intuition, empaths can avoid people with negative energy and form positive relationships. It is important for every Empath to develop his or her intuition. Developing it has a crucial role that will play in helping to form your experience as an empath. It will help to avoid bad energies that may surround you.

#Trait 5 – Aloneness

Empaths always seek to be alone. They often avoid a crowd as a result of the draining effects it often has on them. Being among people is exerting for empaths. They often serve as a healer, dealing with different emotions and feelings. To refuel their energies, they need to be alone: out of sight and other emotions. A short exit from others helps to reload their energy and prevents them from emotional overloads. They often prefer going out in their cars to prevent delays and move freely without distractions. They are like medical doctors that care for others. While they are tending other wounds, they lose lots of strength that require replenishing. The aloneness is the critical time for every Empath to heal himself or herself.

#Trait 6 – Overwhelmed in Intimate Relationship

The high sensitivity rates of empaths affect them in their intimate relationships. They are often affected by closeness; hence, they try to avoid intimate relationships. They usually have a fear of being engulfed in a relationship where they will lose their identities. They usually request a redefinition of the conventional paradigms that explain what a relationship should be and not be.

#Trait 7 – Prone to Energy Draining

Empaths are often victims of energy vampires. Their over-sensitivity to others' emotions makes them liable to others using up their energy. The fear and rage of others are licensed to sap the energy of empaths. Often, energy vampires do more evil than draining empaths' energy physically. Narcissists are dangerous energy drainers. They lack empathy and are selfish in their acts. Their actions can make an empath feel worthless or unlovable. Other possible energy drainer includes chronic talkers, drama queens, victims, etc.

#Trait 8 – Dependent on Nature for Re-energizing

Empaths often replenish their energy through nature. Having fulfilled the demands of the day, empaths seek solace in nature. The duty of alleviating others' feelings and emotions requires a certain filling. Empaths can only give when they are filled. You give what you have. Nature helps to nourish and restore Empath's energy. By replenishing their energy, they get to release their burden and enjoy the company of wild green things, ocean, animals, etc. Their dependence on nature goes in tandem with some of their forms – the fauna and the flora.

#Trait 9 – Highly Tuned Senses

Empaths can be affected by various events, including talking excessively, noise, and smells. This may turn them off. Their lack of interest in these events shows the negative effect of their highly sensitive nature. This is why they often prefer to be alone; they try to avoid crowds and stay with nature.

#Trait 10 – Highly Benevolent

Empaths are givers. They give themselves to others and even give too much sometimes. Empaths are big-hearted. They are always interested in relieving others' pain. Whenever empaths see a needy person, they feel moved to help him or her. They have joy in helping people curb their pain. They even do more than giving. They give and, at the same time, take on the pains and needs as theirs. In the process of helping others, they often end up putting themselves in a needy position that they were not. They care deeply for others and take any possible steps needed to provide for the needs of others.

#Trait 11 – Creativity and Innovativeness

Empaths are creative in all they do. Their minds are never still. They move from one feeling to another emotion. An engaged mind will be effective at whatever it is put into. By having access to many personal issues of others and creating interest in solving their problems, empaths expose themselves to many ideas and practical actions that solve real-time problems. Their minds see the works done on others as projects, and it affects their creativity and innovativeness as human beings.

#Trait 12 – Active Listening skills and Vulnerability

Empaths are great listeners. They show interest in identifying the challenges of others by listening to them. The empathy trait in them makes them show concern over others. Their listening skill gives them access to issues facing others, and they identify possible steps to deal with those issues. However, empaths are vulnerable to being taken for granted by others. Others often take advantage of them. People turn them into a dumping ground and place their challenges on them. They have difficulty saying no to others and end up dealing with other people's challenges.

THE HABITS OF EMPATHS

The term "empathy" has gained the attention of different people and professionals of various fields – scientists and psychologists. Empathy is presently a crucial attitude every teacher of success mentions in his or her teachings. Business leaders now show interest in it and try to utilize it in their organizations to effect change in their employee's effectiveness. Empathy helps to improve our lives and that of other people by understanding their needs and helping them to attain all they need. When you help others, you will gain their respect and expand your sphere of influence beyond your imagination. An empath is a higher form of empathy. It goes deeper and moves from external factors to internal factors to deal with an individual. Empaths are a Highly Empathic Personality. They have certain habits that distinguish them from others. Their characteristics drive these habits. To have a better understanding of empaths, you need to understand their habits. The common actions they are prone to exhibit at any given time. I have seven common habits of empaths here.

#Habit 1 – Curious about Strangers

Empaths are seriously interested in knowing others. They have an insatiable interest to meet a stranger. Highly Empathic people are always ready to start a discussion with others when they meet them. Meeting new people sparks an inquisitiveness in them, which they utilize to satisfy their curiosity. When empaths meet with new people, they do not interrogate but rather show interest in the stranger and want to know about the person by showing interest. They try to understand the person's values, view of life, challenges, interest, successes, and possible ways they can help them achieve all they want. Curiosity has a positive effect on humans. It helps to enhance our life satisfaction and deal with loneliness, which is a long-standing experience among Americans.

#Habit 2 – They Avoid Presumptions and Stay Neutral

Unlike other people who look at the other person's idea and form a notion about him or her without considering general ground and the need to be neutral, empaths are usually generic in their perceptions of others. They do not think of someone as extremist or fundamentalist in any issue. They rather look for a common ground that brings them together with others and judges them based on that. They challenge their prejudices and identify what connects them with others instead of what separates them. Empaths always deal with hatred and find common ground to achieve friendship.

#Habit 3 – They Enjoy Teamwork

When you have an empath as a leader in your workplace, you rest assured that your stay in the organization is filled with successes. They do not think in terms of themselves. They consider the success of the team and speak in "we" and "us." They try to make others feel empowered and supported. Language is a good way to show empathy. It shows how much you care about the other person and your support for his or her challenge. Studies reveal that people who use the second-person pronoun are adept at interpreting others' emotions, feelings, thoughts, and behaviors. Empaths create a connection between them and others by talking about the goals they share. You will hear them make expressions such as: "We can make it work; we only need to get the necessary knowledge and skills." "Don't worry; we will get through this."

#Habit 4 – They Listen and Speak up

The ability of the empaths to put their curiosity into motion lies in two things: their listening skill and openness. Empaths are people that will give you all the attention you think you need. They will not just stop there, but they will also pour out their minds to you. People feel helped when someone cares to listen to his or her plight. They often find solace in it; frequently, it solves their challenges. Empaths help to receive the mind of others about their pains, feelings, and emotions; at the same time, they share their experiences. Usually, they share their experiences to help heal the other person.

#Habit 5 – They Give Inspiration and Enact Social Changes

Empaths are adept at effecting social changes in their society. Empaths use empathy to deal with an issue that pertains to their society. They have the understanding that empathy can serve as a tool to create benefitting changes in society. Activists in history who moved against slavery made use of empathy to achieve the abolition of a slave. As recorded by a journalist, Adam Hochschild, the slave trade abolitionists did not press for their demands by focusing on the written texts but empathy. They tried to make others understand and feel the pain of the slaves on the plantation. Through their campaign, the horrendous experience and the phenomenon were stopped in history.

#Habit 6 – They Give Imaginations to others' point of views

Empaths are perspective takers. This means they do not make a conclusion based on what they see or hear. They consider themselves in the position of others by imagining what steps they would take if they found themselves in a similar situation to what the other person finds himself or herself. It is by their imaginative habit that they can help many. They discover the deficiencies in people and look for ways to help them. You can pick this one habit if you are not an empath. You can cultivate it and empathize with others. You will achieve a lot by helping others and feel satisfied.

#Habit 7 – They use Pauses and Questions

Highly empathetic people utilize the tools of pause and questions to understand others. Many people interrupt or jump to a conclusion before we hear others' opinions. However, Empaths do not interrupt others. They give them attention and listen to their experience before they offer advice. Also, they usually seek clarification before giving their advice. They prefer asking questions to have a better understanding of the other person's points. They often avoid misunderstanding to be able to help others and proffer the appropriate solutions to their emotional challenges.

At times, an empath may not be aware that he or she possesses the super active abilities to help others. You may have heard others say you are an empath, but probably you did not believe it. By going through the characteristics explained above and the habits, I believe you will now have the accurate knowledge to decipher if you are truly an empath. However, if you still have doubts, I have seven events you can check to identify if you are truly an empath.

- Whenever you feel too emotional in some situations and environments, for some, being around a volcano often affects their emotions.
- When others come to you and seek advice
- When you have the urge to be alone from time to time after you mix with others
- When an intimate relationship overwhelms you
- When you feel drained amidst the crowd, you will know this when you have difficulty going to public places such as a mall, parties.
- When you have the urge to sleep alone; except when you have issues with your spouse
- When you take solace in going out of your way to help others: this is common among people.

PART TWO

LIVING YOUR EMPATH'S STATUS

CHAPTER FOUR

EMPATHS AND RELATIONSHIP

Generally, the relationship is an essential aspect of every human. Everyone faces challenges and hills they need to surmount in their relationships. However, empaths have more they need to address. Empaths are highly sensitive people, and they often absorb others' emotions, feelings, and pain. This ability serves as a hindrance to many empaths in their relationships or their decisions to get married. Many empaths try to avoid the closeness of being in a relationship. They are afraid of being engulfed by the feelings of a partner that will always stay close to them from time to time. A part of you wishes that you had a life partner; however, your other part that considers your ability creates fright in you. The truth is that the closer you are to someone, as an empath, the stronger your empath becomes. There is a need to learn how to deal with your ability as an empath to have a successful relationship. I will take you through the realities in an empath's relationship, how an empath can affect his or her relationship negatively, the steps you need to take to balance your ability with your relationship, and finally how your partner can play his or her role to build a strong relationship with you.

THE REALITIES OF AN EMPATH'S RELATIONSHIP

The reality in a relationship that involves an empath is that it is both a curse and a blessing. As much as you are afraid as an empath about the effects of your ability on your relationship, you are right. However, there are other blessings attached to you being in a relationship. You only need to identify the benefits and live by them. Relationships themselves are not easy. It has not been easy for two people to figure out themselves. Now, adding your ability as an empath to the equation will change the activities. It makes the situation more demanding and harder. As an empath in a relationship, you have more to learn to make your relationship work effectively. The first part of an empath's relationship realities is the good or blessing aspect. How is the relationship a blessing?

The Good/Blessing Realities

As an empath in a relationship, you will engage in effective arguments with your partner. For every relationship, the argument is bound to occur. However, the process of expressing it differs from couple to couple. When it is not handled well, it will become a hindrance to the relationship and affect the relationship's progress. Empaths have access to their partner's mind, and they understand how they feel; thus, they have a backdrop on which they will express themselves when they engage in an argument. When an argument occurs, the result is usually positive and better. There is a clear understanding of each other.

The empath's partner will have an understanding of their feelings before they utter a word. You don't need to wait for your partner to tell you his or her mind before you react and take action. This ability helps to curb unnecessary dissension that may want to surface in a relationship because of misunderstanding. In an empath's relationship, it is easy to avoid disagreement and upsetting your partner. You will know he or she needs your attention more and give him or her the needed attention. Imagine your husband coming in late. As an emphatic wife, you will understand what he has gone through and know the best way to treat him now.

There will be a strong bond in your relationship with your partner. Women, especially, love it when their partners care about them and understand their needs. Your ability to know what your partner needs before she asks will help your relationship to grow stronger and bond deeper. Your partner will find it easier to bond and reveal a lot to you. Bonding is an essential element of every relationship. It aids it and takes it ahead.

There will be more happy moments together. In this kind of relationship, the empath does not care about his or her happiness only. He or she is usually after the joy of the partner. This act creates a balance between your experiences of happiness together in a relationship. You enjoy it and have many good memories to share. Good memories shared are great for every relationship, which an empath's relationship does not lack.

The final blessing I have here is the most important blessing any relationship can have – understanding your partner deeply. As an empath, you will have a whole lot of information about your partner, and this often aids your understanding of each other. When you understand your partner and vice versa, it makes your relationship more secure and independent.

The Negative Realities

As an empath, you have access to the total emotions of your partner. When he or she feels happy, you are there in the scenario. However, when negative emotions arise, you are also there. You do not just feel their emotions, but you also reflect it and experience it along with them. The implication of this is that, if your partner is not happy, you will replicate a similar attitude. Honestly, I do not want to imagine how your home will feel on such days.

You do not have control over the emotions. Even if you know it is a negative light, there is less to nothing you can do. It is not a switch that you can turn off and on. It is, at the same time, difficult to ignore.

You need to be part of everything, and you will end up acting in ways you never intended to act.

It is quite a difficult task for an empath to differentiate his or her emotions from the partner's emotions. At times, you are overfilled with your partner's emotion, so you will end up not knowing whose emotion is at work in you. When you are angry, the question is, what is fueling your anger? Your happiness at times, is it yours or the result of another person's emotion on you? It is a good thing to have charge over your emotions and be able to differentiate it from other emotions. However, it is difficult to do that in an empath's relationship.

At times, you tend to want to pretend so that your partner will not know you know how he or she feels. This kind of act will affect you. You will be compelled to act outside your real self. There is little or no space for you to express your emotions.

It is difficult for your partner to lie to you. At times, we should be ignorant of the lies others tell us. As an empath, if your partner lies to you, you will know, and this can affect your relationship. It will affect the trust in the relationship and make you feel less assured of the relationship's future.

HOW EMPATHS AFFECT THEIR RELATIONSHIP NEGATIVELY

The personality of an empath is difficult. It changes your method of relating to others and even to yourself. You will be more concerned about the other person while you may end up denying yourself many benefits. I have identified five possible steps that an empath can take to affect his or her relationship negatively.

Usually, most empaths compromise their boundaries for their partners without their partner's knowledge. In their attempt to help their partners, they often end up leaving behind their emotions, challenges, and deal only with their partner's challenges. It can lead to a misunderstanding between the couple since the partner does not understand what is happening. Stepping into your partner's boundary without her knowledge can lead to anger and resentment, which are inimical to a relationship.

The empaths most times neglect their needs while they cater to the needs of their partner. They often forget their needs, and these needs keep lying fallow without ways to gather and work on them. When their needs are not attended to, the empaths, at some point, will most likely feel unloved and neglected. Their partners also will not be able to help because they lack the understanding of how to meet their needs.

They care less about themselves and only focus on their partner. Empaths are prone to letting go of many things once they are in a relationship. They are likely to stop engaging in the activities they have been engaged in. Sometimes, they stay away from friends, their hobbies, spend less time and energy at work. All these losses can affect their self-esteem and productivity.

Empaths will care for their partners more increasingly daily. When the care gets to a particular stage, the partner may consider it as an intrusion of privacy and feel choked. At this point, when the activities of the empath look like an encroachment on the other partner's privacy, the partner will be stressed out by the encroachment, and this is not appropriate for a healthy relationship.

Empaths usually rely on their minds to solve most issues. When there is an issue that requires attention, empaths would prefer using dialogue in their heads to solve the issues. To the empaths, the issue is resolved; however, the partner will not be aware. This act can lead to a complication because of miscommunication.

BALANCING YOUR GIFT AS AN EMPATH AND YOUR RELATIONSHIP

The relationship for empaths is usually demanding and exerting. It can become a struggle for empaths because they are often lost in the care of others while they end up leaving behind the other person's needs. The challenges in your relationship, as an empath, can be enormous. However, it does not mean you cannot deal with your partner rightly. You only need to be prepared and get ready to make certain moves for your relationship's sake if you are to enjoy your relationship. To have a great experience in your relationship as an empath, you need to get a means to balance it appropriately. You cannot undo your ability, and it will always come into play in any circumstance. However, if you can create a balance, your empathetic ability will work well with your relationship.

Create Boundaries in your Relationship

In a relationship, the world can feel so compacted around your partner. You will most definitely care more for your partner than you care for others. You will always feel all the feelings of the person close to you. However, that feeling of oneness that you see at the beginning of the relationship can cause a hindrance if it is not attended to as soon as possible. When you begin to feel the pains, emotions, and other feelings of your partner, you need to create a demarcation to prevent yourself from being engrossed with her emotions. Being engrossed with her emotions can eventually lead to unhealthiness in your relationship. Find time to care for yourself. Do not always show interest in his or her affairs; that will make it seems like you are choking him or her or being overprotective.

You can be Alright

A common feeling in empaths is their attachment to the well-being of others, which they want to ascertain. They believe that if the other person is not fine, they will not be fine. However, you can be fine, as an empath, even when your partner has challenges. Your happiness is not tied to another's happiness. You only need to take responsibility for caring for others' emotions and pain as if it is yours. Having created a demarcation, understand that you are not responsible for the other person's happiness and joy; you are only a helper in certain cases, and you cannot help them in all other cases. Stick to your lane and help when it is convenient and not too exerting.

Know the Right Time

Many empaths do not know when to say "Yes" to the need of others. You need to know the right time to say No and Yes to others. Sometimes, you need to protect yourself from losing your self-worth and avoid a case of co-dependence. When you say No, you will not depreciate. It does not make you a selfish or a heartless partner. Consider it as a way of creating boundaries in your relationship. You cannot be responsible for the emotional well-being of your partner. Knowing when to say No helps your partner grow independently and increases your relationship's health status.

Use Aloneness

As an empath, the experience of feeling the emotions of your spouse can be so exerting that you will end up using your energy. One right step to take is to disconnect yourself from others. When you are too engrossed with the feeling of your partner, free yourself from the demands by finding time alone. When you are alone, you will create a serene environment for yourself and can ponder on the issues and the best way you can tackle them. During your time alone, reflect on the causes of your burden and identify how you can deal with those burdens. Create a way to avoid such burdens in the coming future.

Understand your Value

More often than not, people celebrate and value you for who you are, not what you can offer them. There are times you will feel shaken and tempted to think you are not loved. You feel like, if you don't show up in every situation, then others will hate or scorn you; however, it doesn't work that way. As an empath, you have beauty, and it lays in the heart of everyone. Being an empath should not weaken your relationship. You need to find the balance that will help you overcome the demands of your relationships and stick by it.

HOW TO DEAL WITH AN EMPATH IN A RELATIONSHIP

I believe, since the relationship is not a broad one-way street, and it involves two-components, the man and the woman, the other partner needs to take specific steps to make the relationship work. When a person who is not an empath enters into a relationship with an empath, the work of making the relationship work does not depend solely on the empath. It ought to be a collective responsibility of the partners involved. If you are not an empath, you need to understand the influence of their sensitivity on their lives. You are required to work in line with them to make the relationship work fine and effectively. You have work to do to make the relationship yield happiness. These are the following contributions you can make to help your relationship with empath result in happiness.

Be Patient

Empaths are humans that are difficult to understand. They have a lot going on within them, and they have many issues to deal with from time to time. You may end up not understanding them at times. However, this does not spell doom. You only need to be patient. There is a crucial power of time; it helps to reveal more hidden facts as time passes. You only need to take your time and understand the empath's plight. The longer you are with him or her, the better you understand what causes his or her actions, and you can easily identify how best to deal with those acts.

Understand their Emotional Struggles

Never forget that empaths have deeper feelings than any other human being does. Their emotions are no longer personal. There is a kind of intrusion in their actions and their feelings. An empath feels more profound than any other person does. The burden of emotions on them makes them stay longer before they can deal with any emotion. When an empath is upset, you need to understand it and bear with him or her.

Establish Effective Communication

Make sure you create a communication atmosphere with your empathetic partner. Always tell your partner how you feel. Avoid making him solve the issues of your emotions his head. When you do not tell your partner how you feel, he has access to the issues; however, he would treat it in his way, which may not be competent enough to deal with it. Tell him or her the way you feel; it will make the process of helping you easier and more effective. It will also help your partner to feel better to speak to you concerning any issues.

Create Space fir Aloneness

Understand that your partner needs to be alone sometimes to help reinvigorate his or her energy. He needs to calm down and check his or her emotions. You need to be supportive by creating time for him or her. At the point when they need to be alone, you will have to sacrifice your wants for them to feel better. If possible, you may help to identify the time you think he or she needs to be alone and help him or her to go into the state to achieve emotional balance.

Appreciate your Empathic Partner

Learn to appreciate your partner. Well, appreciation is a needed element everyone needs to build a strong relationship. Similarly, in your relationship with an empath, you need to replicate it more effectively. Let him or her feel how much he or she is loved. You can show your appreciation with as little as a cup of coffee early in the morning with a kiss and compliment on how good he or she is. When there is no appreciation, your empath partner will feel rejected and used. They may start to hold back their help, and that will affect your relationship.

Avoid lying

Empaths are breathing lie detectors. A costly mistake you can make is to lie to your partner. They can pick up a lie. Usually, their instincts show them when people lie to them. Therefore, do not make them perceive you in the wrong way. Rather, build a good reputation with them and make them respect you for your relationship to be effective and happy.

Make Efforts in the Relationship

Honestly, you have less you can do to help your partner; however, you can still help them in the relationship. Let them feel helped and show concern to them. You do not need to be a perfect helpmate. Try your all to make your partner happy. They appreciate the good gesture as such from their love ones. Give them the attention that shows how much you care and want to offer them your possible assistance. Be a source of inspiration in your dealings with them.

Create Time to be Together

Empaths love it when they get quality time with others. Make sure the time you spend with your partner is emotionally sound. Give him or her the opportunity to be closer to you emotionally. It will affect your relationship more positively than you can think. Spend your meaningful timesharing things together and not just issues that will not benefit you both. In your time together, make him or she understand you and your feelings better. Make sure you get to understand him or her, too, at the possible means you can take to achieve that understanding. When you spend quality time together, your understanding of each other will deepen, and it will aid your relationship and take it forward, then you can think.

Identify What Drains Your partner

Empaths have specific situations and environments that set them off. They can feel drained based on certain circumstances and reactions to those circumstances. The best step to take in dealing with an empath in a relationship is to help identify when your partner often gets drain in his or her emotions. When you identify what drains him or her, it will be easier to help him or her, and this will help to strengthen your relationship.

Know the Source of their Actions

When your partner acts in a way that seems irritating, such as asking you about your day in full detail, this may feel like an intrusion or a form of lack of trust. However, understand that their ability often reveals emotions and feelings. He or she may feel your stress and decide to know the cause to know how to help you. Give him or her the benefit of the doubt and relate your experience. If you are confused and do not know the source of his or her action, you can do well to ask questions. It will help to strengthen your relationship more than you can ever think or imagine.

CHAPTER FIVE

EMPATH AND WORK

Every day, we move from our homes to our place of works. We all have that sense of duty that usually keeps us doing something. We have vacations we want to go on. We want to enjoy life to its fullest and to do all these things; we need to make money. Necessity, truly, is the mother of invention. The knowledge of how much we need makes us go for work that will pay us at the end of the day. However, this work does not come without their demands. Generally, we all face one form of challenge or the other at work. Dealing with these challenges is crucial for us to have a good day at work. As much as we have challenges we face at work, empaths also have their challenges at work. They are plagued with many demands based on their abilities. The requirements of their work often burden them. Their sensitivity often exposes them to much stress attached to the work environment. In this chapter, I will be looking at how empaths react at their workplace, how every empath can prevent the stress and demands they are likely to meet in their workplace. Also, I will look at how empaths can balance their ability with the demands of their workplace and how others can relate with empath at the workplace to achieve an effective and productive result in the work environment.

HOW EMPATHS REACT TO THEIR WORK ENVIRONMENT

The hypersensitivity of empaths affects their work ethics. They act differently from every other person in the work environment. If you are working with empaths, you can get to know why he or she acts the way he or she does. I have identified seven reactions that most empaths exhibit at work.

- **Overwhelming Response to Workload**

Empaths have challenges staying attuned to work when they are saddled with many responsibilities. The fastest means to make an empath useless is to allocate more duty to him or her. They experience a form of a struggle whenever they have more tasks to do than usual. Anxiety often comes in and increases their stress level. They become useless in their morale for work when they have more to do. The overwhelming effects on them reflect on their productivity. It often makes them less productive and creative.

- **Allergic to Noisy Environments**

Many empaths react to open spaces. When at work, they would prefer being alone in an enclosed area where their sensitivity will have fewer emotions and feelings to connect with. Chaotic events usually piss them. Their senses are driven at a higher rate by the sights, smells, sounds, and events that are happening around them. Working in a certain environment, such as a shopping mall where many people walk in to get their list of groceries, will most likely not be palatable for them.

- **Ineffective Under Supervision**

When you place an empath under critical supervision, you will almost end up tying up his or her effectiveness. Empaths are most effective when they work alone with little or no supervision. They feel pressured when they are supervised closely. Empaths do not work effectively under pressure. Once their minds are under pressure, they have quite a lot going on their mind, and many solutions will be hovering in their minds for attention. It often takes their attention away from the job. You may end up not getting the best from the job allocated to them.

- **Observation of others' Discomfort**

Empaths understand the emotions of others. In the workplace, empaths know the needs of their colleagues and offer help. They understand when a fellow worker needs rest or is overloaded with responsibilities. They have access to other emotions. A good reason it is even better to take them away from the public where they will not interact with many people. When many people work around them, it affects their emotions because they are overwhelmed by the various emotions that surround them.

- **The Retreat for Refreshing**

Empaths often go for a retreat to refresh themselves following their exhaustive day at work each day. When they are overwhelmed, they require adequate time to be alone and let go of their stress amassed during the day. Access to a dark room will be a great help to assist them in achieving the calmness they need.

- **Hunger Affects their Effectiveness**

Empaths are often affected by hunger. When they are hungry, they tend to release their anger on others. Hunger affects their functionality and effectiveness. If you are an empath, you need to watch out for this and identify the best means to curb your hunger so you can avoid making enemies at work or reducing your effectiveness.

- **Appreciation for Arts**

Empaths give apt attention to nature, and they appreciate whatever celebrates nature. They give attention to the work of art, music, and appreciate it. Works of art stir up their minds and make them feel emotional. You should not be surprised if you see a colleague who is an empath who reacts to an art exhibition or a musical concert. It only shows his or her personality.

HOW EMPATHS CAN MAKE THEIR WORK EFFECTIVE

Empaths need to be up and doing to make their work experience worthwhile. They need to contribute to its effectiveness. Whether you are going into your business, as an empath, or you are working in a particular organization, you need to prepare your mind ahead and create a balance that will help you deal with the demands of the work environment. If you don't prepare yourself, as an empath for your work, you will end up being frustrated by the demands and the work environment. The workplace is the most vulnerable place. An empath can be plummeted and drained by engaging with various people of varying backgrounds and energies. You need to protect yourself before going to work. Make certain decisions that will help you. Also, while you are at work, you need to take some steps that will help you balance the work's demand with your ability.

Protecting Yourself from Work's Demands

Protecting yourself from the stress and demands of your job, as an empath, is possible. It only requires you to have self-awareness and the will to adopt the strategies you need to protect yourself ahead of the demands.

- Understand your gift and your need: for people to understand you at work, you need to know yourself. Understand the strengths and weaknesses you carry about. Identify your uniqueness and what form of work you need to make it work out effectively. Know how well you can relate with responsibilities and bring about helpful positive results. When you know how well you can relate with the crowd, if you need an enclosed area or not, you will be able to demand it from the organization for your effectiveness.

- Avoid acting like others. Don't try to please them and never try to compare yourself to the other person. If you try to follow another's steps, you will end up frustrating yourself. The way you see things, as an empath, differs from how other people see them. Usually, other people do not understand how you act and why you do what you do. You have a different source of energy and inspiration. Accept the differences between you and others, and you will have peace while you work.
- Learn to speak your mind. This is often a challenge to many empaths. Unless they want to solve other problems, they hardly speak of their emotions and needs. Speaking up in your workplace will help you a lot to prevent misunderstanding and create a palatable working environment for yourself and others. Identify someone open-minded and ready to listen and speak up. Tell them your needs to be able to work effectively at your duty. Be confident as you ask for it. When you speak up, others will be aware of how to help you with your work.
- Plan to care for yourself. You need to plan for your well-being. Regardless of your preparation, you will still be engrossed emotionally in your workplace, except if there are no people around you. However, you should plan how you will deal with the energy you dispense during the day at work by creating a plan for yourself to replenish your strength. Create time to be alone to strengthen your energy. Identify a means of soothing and boosting your energy. Listening to calm music can help. You can also bring nature to your work environment. Plants, flowers will be effective.

Balancing your Gifts and Your Work

Coping with the demands of the work requires some steps. You only need to learn how to centralize yourself between your work and ability without overwhelming yourself with workloads. Your knowledge of your true self and the willingness to set boundaries will aid you in balancing yourself at work.

- Align with your soul and create boundaries before you go into your work. Aligning yourself requires you to understand your real self. Explore your inner ability. Truly, you have an enormous ability in you, as an empath, the ability you have is the fuel of the real you. When you understand your ability, it helps you to work better at work. With the knowledge of yourself, you should create a boundary that will protect you. Thinking that you need to help more people will keep draining you. By aligning with yourself, you will know better how important it is to stay put and know when to help and not to help.
- Avoid attachment in your relationship with others at work. Make it a habit to detach yourself from others in most cases to avoid placing yourself in a dire state where you become overwhelmed. Taking things personally is a common attitude among empaths; however, you don't need to place all the needs of other people on yourself. You need to know when to say yes and say no. You do not try to help deal with all emotional situations. Give yourself a break to be more effective at work.
- Identify the end from the beginning. In your work, there will be many instances when you will feel overwhelmed. A good way to deal with such an occurrence is to create a picture of the end you want to see. It will help to guide your actions

despite the overwhelm. You need to use visualization to build the future you want. Create a mental picture of what you want to see and give it adequate attention. When you focus on what you want to see at the end of the journey, it will make your work easier and feel more compelled to work effectively despite the demands on your ability.

- Utilize your ability to make the work environment better. You also need to use your super-ability to deal with certain situations. Be ready to help others in your workplace. Try to meet with others, discuss, ask questions, and know what they are going through. From the knowledge, use it to help deal with their challenges. Make the world around you in your workplace a better one, but do not do that at the expense of your emotion. When you help them, you will, in a way, save yourself from being distracted and overwhelmed.

DEALING WITH EMPATH AT WORK

This section is for the employers and co-workers with an empath. They also have certain roles to play to bring out the effectiveness of empaths. If you are an employer who has an empath in his or her organization, I have some tips on how you can deal with your empath employee to bring the best out of him or her. Empaths are very creative and talented. However, in the working environment, if they are not well-situated, they will not function effectively. If you can utilize them rightly in your organization, they will produce a great result for your organization and take your organization to the next level of your goals.

#Tip 1 – Make them Autonomous

Empaths work best with little or no supervision. Dare to trust them with responsibilities; they will always come out fine in 9 out of 10 cases. Usually, they may adopt an unconventional approach towards realizing the project you entrust to them; however, the project will be done effectively. One reason it is often important to give them autonomy with less or no supervision is that empaths do not work like others. They require time to chill as they work. During their relaxation, a supervisor may misunderstand it as laziness. However, if you can give them time to chill and work at their pace and comfort, you will get the best of what you desire.

#Tip 2 – Give Clear Direction

Don't make the work complex or ambiguous for an empath. Make it simple and straightforward, and they will surprise you. Empaths are emotional; when details are too complex, they may get into their emotions and affect their perceptions. However, if you allocate little and directly stated work to them, they will be able to carry it out efficiently and effectively. The idea with an empath is to "make it simple." For them, make it simple, and they will bring out the complexities you need from the simplicity.

#Tip 3 – Be an Effective Leader

Avoid being just a boss; be a leader who shows interest in them. Empaths have needs. While taking care of others, most people do not care for them; if you show interest in them, it will be a source of succor to them. As their leader, be emotionally intelligent. Avoid controlling and issuing commands only. It is a primitive form of work ethics. Empaths love bosses that lead effectively and not just managers. They love it when their colleagues in their workplace are leading along with them, not just draining their energies. As a leader, your focus shouldn't be on controlling and getting things done. You need to bring in perspectives and questions the way things are being carried out. Show that you have an interest. Let them see how much you care.

#Tip 4 – Make effective Use of Their Sensitivity

The empaths' greatest strength and ability is their sensitivity. Though many people focus on the demanding aspect of the gift, their sensitivity is a strength that can be utilized effectively by you to get the best out of an empath. Make them more effective by placing them in certain positions that will make them utilize their talent effectively without exerting themselves. You can organize training for them on how they can train their emotions so they will be in charge.

#Tip 5 – Create an Enabling Environment

The environment you provide for an empath will determine how effective he or she will perform. Set them up in a flow-centric climate to be productive and gain restoration. If you want them to be fast at the job you give them, make them work in an environment free of distractions and interruptions. The kind of environment you want to create should be helpful for their effectiveness. It is a good way to make every empath work effectively.

CHAPTER SIX

UTILIZING YOUR SPIRITUAL GIFTS RIGHTLY

Being an empath is a state of being. It is more of a nature that some people have. Not everyone is an empath. We have them in our world walking and working among us. Survey studies have revealed that 20 percent of our population is made of empaths. The distinguishing factors of empaths are in their gifts – spiritual gifts. Not everyone has these gifts. It is only found in these few people. If you are an empath, it simply means you have the gifts that only 20 percent of our population have. Every empath is one naturally. It is not what you seek to achieve or train yourself to become. The spiritual gifts of empaths are designed to lighten our world and help many from their state of helplessness. It is a good thing to have people among us who can heal our inner sicknesses without asking us to pay. Sometimes, empaths help the people around them without their knowledge.

Nonetheless, as an empath, you need to protect yourself and utilize your spiritual gift rightly. If you lack the adequate and right knowledge on how to utilize your gifts appropriately, you will become ineffective. Every empath is prone to bad energies and other draining factors. These draining factors are waiting to sap your energy, and this is only possible when you fail to utilize your spiritual gift rightly. I will explain the steps you need to take to use your gifts rightly. However, before the information on how to utilize your gifts, I will take you through the gifts themselves.

THE EMPATH'S BASIC GIFTS

The Gift of Vision

Empaths are endowed with the eye of the bird. They have access to things around them without necessarily going through any social media platforms, such as google, twitter, yahoo, Facebook, etc. Empaths are capable of knowing every difficult symbol that any situation may have. They have access to what happens in their bodies or that of other people, in their businesses and the world, with a clear understanding of all activities. With their visionary ability, they can identify issues of minute consequences and pay attention to the most important ones. With the gift of vision, they make good leaders who have the ability to project into the future and do what is right for the benefit of the community.

The Gift of Intuition

Intuition is a general gift in our word. We all have the gut feeling that we get without any cognitive reasoning. However, the gut feeling of empaths is deeper. Caroline Myss, the author of "Anatomy of the Spirit," explains intuition by linking it with the plexus chakra – Manipura, which is the stronghold that holds the empath's self-respect and self-esteem. The chakra contains the key to empath's protection from physical danger – survival intuition. The survival intuition gives them a signal when negative energy approaches. The strength of the gift of intuition depends on the empath's ability to have a strong sense of respect for themselves and others. Self-esteem is also important. It empowers every empath to gain control over the maintenance of his or her body's health. The lack of self-esteem will affect the intuition of empaths.

The Gift of Psychic

Empaths are physically attuned, aside from being emotionally inclined to others. With the gift of psychic, an empath can get a feeling about a person from miles away and possibly sense some of their experiences that are not palatable. The psychic gift works in such a way that the empath will get a signal about someone. It may be his or her customer, friend, or family member. The empath may see the person's face, hears his or her name, and most will most likely feel uneasy in his or her intuition. The empath's psychic gift often presents someone's feeling in the form of an energy feeling. It sometimes makes the empath looks like a medium. The gift only depends on the ability of the empath to follow the signal and make meaning out of it. It requires the empath to trust the signal.

The Gift of Presence

When empaths are around other people, there is a kind of illumination that occurs in others. Through their presence, others receive healings to their various emotional pains and feelings. Empaths have a strong ability to stay with people. However, the effectiveness of this gift depends greatly on the frequency of its use. The presence of empaths serves as a tonic for healing the different mental illnesses of others.

The Gift of Healing

Empaths are natural healers. They can heal themselves and others. One of the reasons empaths are prone to overwhelming experience is their healing gift. The gift situates them in a position where they find it difficult letting others go without identifying a means of solving their mental pain. To heal someone, empaths often do the processing and healing in their minds. They have the feeling of making the world beautiful by making everyone live without pain or any form of sadness. Empaths can heal their hearts and that of others, and with the healing, they transform their bodies and that of others. As an empath, you need to start using your power to heal yourself.

The Gift of Creativity

Empaths are highly creative. They are adept at designing, art, filming, architecture, marketing, teaching, etc. They are experts at changing abstract ideas into tangible success. If you have a dream as an organization, an empath can help you realize the dreams in no time. Their creativity works in line with the gift of vision. Also, their creative gift helps them to proffer all forms of solutions to different problems of others they want to solve.

HOW TO UTILIZE YOUR GIFTS RIGHTLY

Empaths are like a sponge that soaks up all the emotions and energy that come around them. They possess an impressive ability. However, it requires knowledge to be able to utilize it correctly. If it is not used rightly, there are certain steps back that an empath will suffer. The empath may end up soaking up negative energy, depression, insomnia, anxiety, and many others. Fortunately, there are ways you can, as an empath, use your empathic abilities in the right way, such that it will benefit the other person and you.

Recreate negative feeling

As an empath, you are prone to various forms of feelings. Your gift does not possess the ability to sieve bad energy from good energy. You need to be aware of it personally and know the necessary steps to take. Whenever you attract negative energies to yourself, it is best to reform it into good energy. How do you do this? You need to think of the energy you received as information. The increase in the information at your disposal will lead to an increase in your intelligence and ability to deal with situations and solve issues. With the stack of information at your disposal, you will have enough resources to address the different problems as they surface. To use the information rightly, you need to incorporate your emotional intelligence.

Deal with Every Issue before They Go Extreme

Taking up others' problems is quite a pain. Nonetheless, it is not bad. It is a way to help others deal with their challenges. When you observe a terrible feeling in others, make sure you attend to them as soon as possible. Take up problems when they are still budding and deal with them accordingly before they escalate into significant issues. For instance, if you observe animosity between two of your children, utilize your ability to treat the issue before it grows out of hand. You may even prepare yourself for a fallout in case it occurs.

Similarly, immediately, you observe a negative feeling hovering around your mind, take caution, and deal with it promptly. Prevent it from growing out of hand. It is like saying, "Prevention is better than cure."

Create Effective Relationships

One way to use your gift effectively, as an empath, is to create effective relationships. For existing ones, you should work on them and improve them. When you observe that a friend of yours is having issues with you but has failed to speak up, you should address the issue as soon as possible. Act on other people's vibes and energy as soon as it is needed. Make sure you set up a platform where the people around you will be free to air their grievances toward you, and you will solve all to build up your relationship strength. When you surround yourself with well-developed relationships, your empathic abilities will work effectively because it is safe from any form of negative energy.

Develop your Relationship at Work

Two factors influence our lives significantly: our relationships at home and our work environment, including our relationships at work. Once we enter into the world and start working, we spend most of our days in our workplace and our weekends with family members and friends. These two factors affect our lifestyle and experience. As an empath, you need to improve your relationship at work as much as you will enhance it outside work. The work environment can be tumultuous and stressful sometimes. It is not an easy task to work with different people on the same team. You must establish a strong relationship with the people in your workplace so you can get to know them effectively. If you lack adequate information about others because of an unhealthy relationship, you are prone to picking up different energies from people in the office. You may pick up anxiety, depression, etc. from coworkers. However, your knowledge of the people around you will shield you from unwanted energy in the office. Similarly, it will aid your relationship with them.

Prepare for the Days Ahead

The world does not give happiness all the time. There are times people change. An environment you are used to will become alien on such days; your workplace may become hostile. Be prepared ahead of those days. Prepare your mind and avoid letting such days meet you unnoticed. As an empath, you can decipher when things are working fine and when they are not. If you sense hostility from your partner or your work environment, quickly adopt the best solution to the situation to avoid hurting your energy. Have a second plan; don't permit bad news to meet you unaware. In your preparation, you should plan to move on when the worst happens. It can be devastating to lose one job or break a relationship. However, with your ability to foresee the imminent evil, it will be easier for you to increase the timeline of your recovery from the blow it gives to you. You need to know that the method or technique you used to deal with a challenge is not as important as how you move on and learn from the challenge.

Always Be Ready to Help Others

This may sound like repetition, or perhaps like I am begging the question. Of course, it is the primary skill of every empath to deal with others' feelings and help heal them. However, you need to make good use of your gift. Imagine you getting a sharp hoe and keeping it in the yard. The scraper is sharp and can cut through any grass. However, your failure to make use of it will dampen it, and it may rust and lose its vitality.

Similarly, if you fail to help other people to heal their emotional pains and feelings, those feelings will end up escalating into viruses and negative vibes. Interestingly, you will end up coming in contact with them, and each time that happens, the feelings your empathic skill will absorb will be those rotten emotions of pain. Aside from the happiness and joy that abound in helping others solve their problem, you would have solved many possible problems that are likely to surface in you.

Create an Understanding from other's Feeling

If you want to use your skill effectively and get a good result, you need to go beyond absorbing other's emotions. It is easier for empaths to be aware of other people's emotions and pain. However, it is quite difficult for many of them to understand the pain they know. As an empath, you need to have an understanding of the pain. When you understand them, you will know the best approach to deploy, which will deal with the problem effectively.

The ability every empath possesses is not enough if it is susceptible to consistent draining. You need to have an effective means of protecting it against the wiles of the surrounding environment. You are prone to bad energies, wrong perceptions from people, and others. You need to protect yourself against others and live your gift out effectively. Empaths find themselves in different fields and professions. We have them as nurses, healers, teachers, and massage therapists. They possess nurturing and loving energy. By following the tips above, you do not have to be afraid of utilizing your gift. Neither will you be subjected to the fear of being drained unnecessarily. It will be easier for you to mingle with others and relate with them without any burden.

PART THREE

PROTECTING YOURSELF AND GIFT

CHAPTER SEVEN

UNDERSTANDING NEGATIVE ENERGIES

Everyone emits certain energy whenever others are with them; these energies are also auras. While some people give positive auras or energy, some give negative energy. The positive energy is laced with happiness, strength, activeness, and every other positive experience. However, the negative gives otherwise. The negative energy often turns a person down and places him or her in a bad position. Negative energies are hindrances to the effectiveness of empaths. Negativity is prevalent in the world, and it is one main challenge faced by empaths. Negative energy creates the feeling of heaviness, gloominess, darkness, defensive acts, with a different view of the world in a negative manner. When empaths are engulfed with negative energy, they become exposed to the mixed filter of anger, fear, and paranoia. The effects of negative energies are often felt both mentally and physically because of the connection that exists between the body and the mind. The body of empathy will experience certain health challenges, including increased blood pressure, an increase in the level of adrenaline and cortisol, shallow breathing, and tense muscles.

Negative energy is toxic to an empath. It does no good. As an empath, you may be able to manage the negative energy; however, you will be drained over time. There is a need to stay away from negative energy. It affects an empath. The negative energies from others will hinder the positive energies. Usually, the source of negative energies for empaths is other people who carry negative feelings and belief systems. For empaths, there are different types of negative energy they are prone to. I have identified six types of negative energies found among empaths.

TYPES OF NEGATIVE ENERGY

Stress and Anxiety

Empaths are often exposed to stress and anxiety. They get these from people around them. Most people today are subject to stress and anxiety. Some have invested in the stock market, and they have no other interest apart from daily reading about the stock market. This often creates fear, anxiety in such people. Stress often emanates from anxiety. Empaths are human on this earth. They walk with their two legs, and they are exposed to other people, including those suffering from anxiety and its consequence – stress. When an empath permits anxiety to have a place in himself or herself, it affects his or her positive energy and builds up to fear. This combination affects the mental health of empaths and distracts them from being effective at work or in their relationships. The most devastating truth is that the bad energy of stress and anxiety cannot be left alone without proffering a timely solution to curb it. When the empath leaves stress and anxiety, they will work hard to produce additional negative energy, which will affect an empath.

Bad Moods and Depression

Depression is another common negative energy empaths prone to. It has enormous effects on empaths, both mentally and physically. Bad moods and depression affect the effective thinking skills of a person, including an empath. They affect the socialization of empaths and give empaths a bad face in public. Depression often affects the empath's emotions and overwhelms him or her. Moving close to those who are depressed is the fastest means of coming in contact with this negative energy. As an empath, the process of absorbing other's emotions is the likely point where you would encounter depression. One magnificent feature of depression and bad moods is their ability to rub off on another person. If you move close to depressed people without proffering the appropriate solution, you will end up becoming depressed. Depression affects the effectiveness of an empath to help others because the empath is fully engaged already.

Habitual Faultfinding

The habit of finding fault always occurs in terms of consistent complaining by an empath. Our world is filled with many deficiencies that require attention. We all have a thing to complain about. The ineffective payment method in our work may be one; the lack of effective tools to carry out our duty at work can also catch our attention and make us complain. Many things are not working right in a society that we want to condemn and criticize. Doing things once in a while and proffering the necessary solution to them is not wrong. However, constant pondering on these issues with a lamentation about them is an ineffective method of dealing with such issues. This is negative energy because it shifts the attention of a person from the solution to a problem but focuses on the person's attention on the problem. This is why empaths need to analyze the problem they want to solve carefully, and the personality involved. Constant complaint sends people away from a person. Others will not be portrayed rightly. The negative energy often affects relationships of empaths.

Physical Ailments

Physical sicknesses can be transferred as a form of negative energy from others to empaths. Empaths are usually exposed to many sick folks. The law of attraction works right with them. By nature, empaths are healers, hence the need for them to have more contact with sick people than any other person. The reaction of an empath toward sick people determines the result of whether they will absorb the negative energy of their sicknesses or not. When empaths meet with sick people, the best action is to examine the person's situation and help critically. However, during the process of extending their hand of help to the person, empaths need to be careful of the negative energy of the sick person. An empath should never forget to take care of himself or herself while taking care of the other person. The physical ailment energy is reflected in forms of muscle pain, headaches, loss of sleep, and many more.

Relationship Problems

Relationship challenges are often one of the negative energies that many empaths have to deal with. Generally, most empaths are afraid of relationships. They have a fear of getting too involved in the relationship, and as such, they often want to try to avoid it. More than their personal experience concerning relationships, other people who suffer from emotional breakdown usually come to such a state following an issue in their relationships. Relationship problems are one of the causes of the pain in many people, and the exposure of many empaths to these issues can rub off on them if they do not carefully relate with those who have the challenge. Empaths are so compassionate that they may end up taking up the feeling of another person as if it is theirs. The relationship problem starts by taking the empath away from his or her friends and loved ones.

Draining Environments

Some environments are poisonous to empaths. Empaths are attached to environments. An environment with positive energy will always balance an empath. It gives the empath the required strength to carry out his or her healing duty. However, negative energy environments turn off an empath. The empath feels drained and low. Such an environment usually gives an empath emotional instability. Draining environments are places filled with people with negative thoughts. There is a kind of hatred or displeasure attached to the environment, and the displeasure will affect the way empaths will perceive the environment and make meaning of it.

EMPATHS AND DEPRESSION

Among the six negative energies, depression is one of the commonest negative energies that most empaths encounter. When empaths are not able to leave the environment that gives them stress to be alone to replenish their energy, they will be exposed to depression. There is a way the environment of empaths overstimulates them. Their sensitivity to other people's actions and emotions also make them vulnerable. Empaths are vulnerable to depression for several reasons.

- **Vulnerability to Sensory overload**

Empaths are exposed to absorbing more sensory information. They have a higher frequency of experiencing information than others, and they have deeper feelings of emotions than an average human being does. The result of this is that open places and noisy environments easily overwhelm empaths. The need to be at work can be a limiting factor that prevents empaths from leaving such environments. In such instances, the empaths enter into depression. The many people they usually carry daily require a lot of energy from them, which they need to replenish by having time alone. When the time to be alone becomes impossible, depression sets in and becomes negative energy at work.

- **Vulnerability to Physical overload**

Just as they are vulnerable to sensory overload, empaths are also sensitive to their physical environment. They are sensitive to the feeling in their bodies. Empaths are allergic to certain foods and drinks. Some empaths have a high rate of sensitivity when it comes to caffeine, prescription drugs, or household cleaners. The sensitivity affects their minds. They tend to believe there is something wrong with themselves, and since people have difficulty understanding them, they do not get enough sympathy, which propels their thoughts about their bodies. The feeling they have will eventually lead them to depression.

- **The Loads of Pain on Them**

Another contributing factor is their taking over others' emotions directly as if it is theirs. They often pick up others' emotions, and when they lack adequate knowledge on how to deal with people, it will be difficult for them to identify negative emotions that they are not to absorb. During the period of absorbing the emotions of others, empaths are likely to take on some negative emotions, including anger and depression. There is the challenge of identifying the emotions that belong to the empaths from those that they absorb. The knowledge of this will help to deal with depression and many other negative energies.

- **The Feeling of Low Self-esteem**

Most empaths are liable to think that something is not right about them. When they do not know how their abilities work, there is always the feeling of alienation from others. Their feeling of low self-esteem comes from the fact that their feelings and emotions do not work like that of other people. Moreover, at times, others may consider them as being shy or needy. When people have these notions about them, they feel rejected and inherently flawed. They lack trust in themselves. Whenever a person lacks trust in himself or herself, the feeling of self-doubt, low self-esteem, and shame will set in. Low self-esteem often leads to depression and social anxiety. There is a need to educate most empaths, so they will have a full understanding of how their brains work. Their brains work quite differently from other's brains. Also, their introversion as individuals can affect their perception of themselves. With many people walking freely and speaking out, empaths can start having the feeling that they do not fit into our world, and this may lead them to withdraw further into depression. The differences in our brain functionality affect the way we see things, and it does not mean they are lowly, shy, or needy. Understanding this fact is what most empaths need. Similarly, empaths are useful in many organizations. If they can accept who they are and value their gifts through their unique abilities, including intuition, empathy, and perceptiveness, the organizations they found themselves in will thrive in no time.

EMPATHS AND INSOMNIA/FATIGUE

Having worked through the whole day treating and healing diseases, empaths are prone to the risk of adrenal fatigue. Adrenal fatigue is exhaustion that includes different symptoms such as body aches, stress, anxiety, insomnia, inability to think clearly. The cause behind this is the inability of the adrenal gland to keep up with the stress from outside. The inability of the gland results in the depletion of cortisol – a hormone that helps to keep our body energized. The ability of empaths to take on the feelings of others affects them and adds to their stress level, and this makes them more vulnerable to insomnia. I have some what I call quick-fix measures you can take as an empath to deal with your adrenal fatigue. These measures are not to fix it permanently. You need to do more than follow these measures. You need to follow a basic lifestyle, using the techniques I will take you through in the next chapter.

My Quick-Fix Measures to Empath's Insomnia and Fatigue
- Measure your cortisol level through a blood test and work on replacing your natural cortisol temporarily by following your doctor's suggestion.
- Give yourself a restful sleep. Make sure you rest daily.
- Create boundaries between yourself and the energy vampires.
- Give yourself to eating a whole food diet. To achieve the whole food diet, you can drop low-quality salt and go for Himalayan salt (seek your doctor's suggestion if you have high blood pressure), stay away from white flour, watch and minimize your sugar intake.
- Give yourself to exercise. It will help to build your stamina and challenge you.

- Meditation is key. Through meditation, you will be able to replenish yourself.
- Practice positive thinking. You may even use affirmations. Avoid building up negative thoughts in yourself but, rather, think positively about every situation.

Negative energies are easy to identify. However, they are quite demanding to deal with. Eliminating negative energy requires techniques that can prevent empath's minds from processing the alluring sight of negative energies. In the next chapter, I will discuss the techniques every empath can adopt to deal with negative energies.

CHAPTER EIGHT

TECHNIQUES TO DEAL WITH NEGATIVE ENERGIES

Empaths are daily emotion absorbers. They are into the habit of helping others, and they do this by picking up the emotions of other people. These activities often drain empaths of their energy. It affects their overall functionality. It will be an anathema for a healer to be sick. If you do not take care of your positive energy, the negative energy carriers around you will influence you and gather all their negativities into you. You need a protective measure against every negative energy that may come near you. The truth is you cannot live without coming in contact with negative energies, but you can live without the influence of the energies. I have identified three basic methods you can use to deal with negative energies. Whether you want to protect yourself against it, or you want to clear your mind of negative energy, these techniques will always prove to be worthy. The process of clearing and dealing with bad energy is not easy. It is demanding and exerting. However, it is not impossible. Taking the right step will surely help to deal with every negative energy a person may have around him or her. The three techniques I plan to discuss are:

- The Shielding Technique
- The Grounding Technique
- The Clearing Technique

THE SHIELDING TECHNIQUE

Every empath functions like a vibrational instrument that vibrates to the tune of others' thoughts and feelings. The feeling of pity an empath has toward a person who has emotional pain often leads to the empath's relapsing into negative energy. Empaths become worried once they leave a person when they just discovered his or her pain. They become engrossed with how to help the individual and heal him or her.

Shielding is like the use of an umbrella to protect yourself from the downpour of rain. It is a form of protection against harsh and negative energy. When you can shield yourself effectively, you would have protected yourself from unclean energy that is capable of ruining your day and making you useless. It keeps your energy tone on a high-level without blemish. Shielding yourself will protect you in a work environment where competition is high, and all forms of negative thoughts are flying around. People with negative energy around you will not be able to deposit it in you. It is as if you are under a covering. The shield's technique protects you easily in any situation. When you find yourself beside an energy vampire, all you need to do is put on your shield. I have the following methods for you to shield yourself from bad energy each time you are amid energy vampires.

Methods to Shield Yourself from Negative Energy

- **Adopt Distractions**

The reason most empaths are prey to negative energy is that they are too focused on the need to absorb other emotions. While they are busy dealing with other problems, they often create an avenue for negative energies to permeate into them. Creating distractions will be an excellent way to help prevent them from giving room to negative energy. Try to avoid yourself when you see the information that may hinder your positive vibe. The way to create distractions includes creating a complicated math problem in your head. You may even create a mental picture of an object between you and the approaching information. The object you want to visualize needs to be something alluring to you. Something that will easily take your mind off the approaching negative energy could be a celebrity face or a flora if you are given to plants as an empath.

- **Strengthen Your Shield Defense**

It is not enough to utilize distractions. You need to make your shield stronger by using a more effective visualization of a wall or defense field surrounding you. Pick up a glowing egg of energy (your favorite color) and imagine it. Your ability to create a vivid mental picture will determine how strong your defense will be. Can you create a picture that seems real in front of you? When you set the field of defense with your imagination, make sure you design it to keep off any form of information you don't want to receive. With gradual practice, you can make it allow just a specific kind of information. I mean, by training your mind to protect you against negative energy, at a certain point, it will automatically shut down when negative energy tries to permeate. When you can achieve this, there will be less competition for your attention. Stay on a stronger visualization, and you can get the relief you need.

- **Incorporate Your Subconscious Mind**

Using your subconscious mind can be quite demanding and challenging; however, it is more effective than you think. Rather than using visualization to create a shield around yourself, you can utilize your internal power of feeling. You do not need to create any mental image. All you need to do is to control the type of field you create around yourself by utilizing meditation. The subconscious mind is quite effective as an option for shielding yourself. However, it is more needed to prevent a mental assault.

- **Utilize Crystals**

You can make use of crystals to protect yourself from negativity. Crystals are minerals that are powerful and effective in solving energy issues. The minerals include stones, rocks, and gemstones. These stones help to protect and magnify different energies. If you can have these crystals on you, wearing or keeping it close to you in your office will help you to prevent negative energy from surrounding and influencing you. Some of the crystals you can use are:

The Amethyst: A beautiful purple gemstone helps to lift the energy around you and in you.

Obsidian: A black stone that deflects negativity, such as anger and psychic attacks

Citrine: A yellow stone that helps to increase positive energy and prevent negative energy

Clear quartz: It refracts sunlight into rainbows and follows a similar process in dealing with negative energy by breaking it up and turning it around.

Smoky quartz: This crystal helps to release negative energy from past relationships while a person sleeps. You need to place it near your bed.

Rose quartz: It is a pale pink crystal, and it helps to protect you in romantic relationships.

Lapis lazuli: It is a blue stone that gives general protection.

The shielding technique will only deal with mental intrusions and prevent your mind against negative energy. There is possible physical related negative energy, and to deal with those, you need to utilize another technique.

THE GROUNDING TECHNIQUE

Grounding involves you placing your consciousness within the confines of your body. You do not allow your consciousness to float over your body. Frequently, people leave their bodies and the world in their mental realm. They often do this during the dream period and in a meditative state. However, when a person is awake, he or she needs to understand that he is in the body actively and should conform to how the body relates.

Grounding involves you connecting your body with the earth. It is often helpful for you, as an empath, to connect yourself with the earth's energy. Grounding can be done in different ways. Crystals can be used, diet can be of help, and some physical exercise can be of good means. Grounding wants you to connect with nature and release enough energy that will help you fight against negative energy. Use the following approaches to ground yourself effectively.

- **Incense and Oil**

In the past, the culture of grounding oneself was based on the use of incense and oils, and the act is still predominant among native Americans today. The natural fragrance that comes from herbs, such as sweetgrass, juniper, sage, pine needles, and cedar, helps to cleanse bad energy. They also help to activate the mind for positive energy and increase the empath's sensitivity to attract surrounding positive energy. The oil and incense need to be one hundred percent based on nature. It should lack any form of adulteration. If it is only natural, it is very effective in dealing with negative energy. You can burn the incense in your house to have an atmosphere that supports your energy.

- **Utilize the Power of Water**

There is a natural power in water that can help to soothe the pain of empaths. Water can help to wash away the negative energy that surrounds you, and there are many ways you can make use of water to ground yourself against negative energy. You can take a bath or shower; as you do so, you should focus on the flow of the water through your body. You may go for a swim, or perhaps place yourself near a body of water and observe it as you reflect on your thoughts and the negative energies that surround you. You can also make use of water as part of the decoration in your home; this includes setting up an aquarium or a fountain near you. It will help you to experience daily grounding.

- **Adopt Meditation**

The effects of meditation on a person's mind are numerous. Either in your house or at the workplace, you should find time for yourself to be alone and reflect deeply on your thoughts. Meditation helps to center a person's thoughts. Meditation enables you to clear your mind of negative influences. As an empath, you have loads of emotions and feelings on your mind. One way to let them go is to engage in meditation. When different emotions from different people come in, they are combined with your emotions, which make you have more emotional loads than an average person. The possible result is confusion. Through meditation, you can cut through the emotions while you clear your mind of those that are not yours. Make it a practice to find a time to meditate and clear your mind of junk.

- **Make Use of Gems and Stones**

Crystals are also useful in the process of grounding yourself. Their usefulness stems from their naturalness. They are products from the earth; hence, they will help to create a fusion between your body and the earth. You can carry the stones in your purse. They are quite small. You may wear yours as jewelry. You only need to ascertain that the gemstone is purely natural without adulteration. Aside from taking them around you, you can use the gemstone by holding them and rubbing them whenever you feel the negative energy around you. During your meditation, you can also hold them close.

- **Have a Date With Nature**

Communing with nature is one of the best ways to ground yourself. Identify your favorite spot and create the time to be with nature. Make sure the location is quiet and conducive. While you are alone, you can say what you want to say aloud. To have a date with nature, you need to utilize all your senses, sight, hearing, smell, taste, and touch. See it as a kind of treat and be the best you can while at it. You may use a natural sunscreen, bug spray, specific dress for the weather, depending on the period of the year and your choice of location. Watch out if the weather will not be too harsh; prepare ahead to avoid distraction from nature while you try to seek solace from it.

- **Walk Barefooted**

This is the most common and most basic grounding method there is. It is quite simple. All it requires you to do is to take off your shoes and walk barefooted; the purpose is to feel the earth. As an empath, feeling the earth beneath your feet will tremendously help your health and keep your emotions at bay. It helps to rebalance the emotional state of empaths. You may do it in your house in the backyard or perhaps go to the beach.

- **Cut the Cord**

A connection occurs between every empath and the other person each time they absorb someone's emotion. As an empath, you establish the connection, which is also a cord. Depending on the type of emotion and energy you absorb, the cord can be positive or negative. When the emotions are negative, the cord you create will be negatively inclined to permit the flow of the negative energy from the other person to come into you. One way to free yourself is to cut the cord that connects you. You will cut out the cord by severing relationships that are not healthy. When you do that, you will have protection over your energy and free yourself from negative energy.

THE CLEARING TECHNIQUE

The clearing technique involves you dealing with the negative energy that exists in your mind. You can consider the technique as another possible method you can use to clear your mind of bad energy feeding on you. Aside from shielding and grounding your energy, you can clear the energy and live an effective life that succeeds in all it does. Below are the methods you can adopt to clear negative energy from you as an empath.

- **Hand Washing**

Hand washing affects you. Each time you engage in hand washing, you are cleaning your energy and getting rid of negative influence. You only need to use soap and some warm water for cleaning.

- **'Internal and External Cleansing Ritual**

A water cleansing ritual helps to balance the energy center of empaths, which is their sacred chakra. Practicing the ritual is possible in two ways: while you drink water (Internal cleansing) and during your bath (external cleansing). Internally, drink a glass of water with attention, mindfulness. Then, visualize the cleansing process going on in you internally. To carry out the ritual externally, when you take your bath or take a swim, you need to pay attention to the cleansing and the process of purifying your energy by the effect of the water on different parts of your body. The cleansing ritual requires both water and the power of visualization.

- **Salt and Oil**

After your day at work or with friends when you have exhausted your energy on others, it is always best for you to have a salt shower. A salt shower implies you are adding Epsom or sea salt in your shower. You can also mix the salt with shampoo. You should make this a regular practice, especially after your daily routine when you have met a lot of people with internal struggles. Oils such as lavender and sage will also be of help to help heal the negative energy surrounding you. Add the oil into your shower or bathtub and take a relaxing bath.

- **Clean Your Space Energy**

Purifying your physical space energy is important for you to cleanse your energy from negative energy. Your physical environment can have an impact on your energy. If it is not well-saturated, it will affect your energy and weigh you down. Purifying your environment requires a simple step. Fill a bowl with water and add two tablespoons of sea salt to it. Then, place the bowl in the corner of your room or office. Leave the bowl for a whole night. The salt in the water will absorb the old energy in the space. When you remove the water the following day, you are taking away the old energy. It is a good technique you can practice daily to keep your energy afloat against impeding energies.

- **Stay Away From Noise and Meditate**

Learning to detach yourself from noise is essential if you want to protect yourself from negative energy. Identify the best time to deal with others and the chaos around you. Stay away from them and find the best time to relax your mind. Immersing yourself in nature will help you regain the energy you lost to help others. Use the time you separate by giving yourself to meditation. Meditation is very effective in dealing with your energy.

- **Set Good Boundary**

As empaths, you need to keep away from people who drain your energy. As much as you want to help others, you should not do that at the expense of your energy. When you are dealing with someone, make sure you only treat the person and stay away from him or her. Your interactions with people of negative energy need to be at the barest minimum. You are not to take responsibility for the pain of other people. Once you apply your ability to heal, know when to stay away, and keep away.

CHAPTER NINE

DEALING WITH ADDICTIONS

The high rate of sensitivity of empaths makes them become overwhelmed and overstimulated. They take on more emotions than an average human being does, and this affects their minds. It is like a burden on them. When the feeling is too much on them, they often resort to self-medication. Their self-medication is usually attempted toward healing themselves of their overwhelming feelings and reaching a status of freedom in their minds. To make their feelings disappear and keep their thoughts calm, they try to numb themselves. In the process of their self-medication, empaths run into addiction. Their natural duty and its negative impacts make them prone to addictions. Addiction relates to dopamine – the hormone that increases the happiness feeling in a person. The negative energies that empaths battle lead them to indulge in certain acts to relieve the pain they get.

Empaths feel other people's emotions and feelings. No doubt, they help to amplify the good vibes in others, and this is the reason others try to locate them and seek their support. They serve as the lifeline for others. However, empaths can be like a foolish guard that left his house wide open while he safeguards other houses. Empaths can absorb others' negativity, hence the beginning of their exposure to addiction. Addiction occurs to an empath when he or she does not have adequate knowledge on how to deal with his or her overwhelming situation.

HOW ADDICTION WORKS

The science of addiction begins with the human brain. The brain is involved in the recording of all pleasures in the same manner. It does not sieve the source of the pleasure, whether it is from reward from others, sexual activity, a delicious meal, psychoactive drugs, or exposure to social media. The brain considers all as pleasures and regulates them, having registered them as the same. The brain gives a different signature to pleasure. Pleasure is based on the release of the neurotransmitter dopamine that is in the nucleus accumbens, which is a cluster of nerve cells that lie under the cerebral cortex. Empaths are naturally endowed with central nervous system sensitization. The existing studies concerning addiction state that dopamine interacts with another neurotransmitter, glutamate, to take over the system of the brain reward-related learning. When a person is addicted to a particular substance or behavior consistently, it causes the person's nerve cells located in the nucleus accumbens and the prefrontal cortex – the area of the brain that is involved in planning and executing tasks to have a communication that creates a state of likeness with desiring to have it; this communication is what leads many addicts to go after the substance they are addicted to.

THE EFFECTS OF ADDICTION ON EMPATHS

There are several effects of addiction on empaths. You can consider those effects the price for it. Usually, empaths are given to certain addictions that relate to sex, love, internet, gambling, gaming, shopping, etc. The effects of these addictions are felt on the body, mind, and spirit of empaths. Addictions wear down their bodies, make their minds inactive, and affect their spirit's effectiveness. This creates several illnesses, including depression and anxiety. Addiction only gives you short-term relief from every sensory overload that you may have. However, it will fade after a while. When it fades, you will come back to your previous state of overwhelming feelings at a higher rate.

HOW TO KNOW IF YOU'RE ADDICTED

- **Create Self Awareness**

A perfect step to take if you want to know whether you are addicted is to create self-awareness; there is liberation in knowing oneself. You should not be ashamed of yourself or blame yourself. Knowing how addictive you are will help you to gain accurate knowledge into how best you can appreciate your reaction to your empathic abilities. When you know your status concerning addiction, it will become easier for you to deal with it. Self-awareness will help you to identify the type of addiction you have. Many people, including empaths, have little or no knowledge about themselves. This is the bedrock of most challenges they face. As empaths, your abilities to know the other person's emotions and challenges should be driven toward identifying yourself.

- **Evaluate Yourself**

Many empaths are not aware of their addiction. Some even think that the behavior they engage in is a way of replenishing the energy they used. Many empaths are undiagnosed, and as a result, they are not aware of how the overstimulation and high sensitivity propel their addiction. As empath, you need to know whether you have your sensitivity under control and ask yourself how you are coping with it. There are certain ways you can know whether you need to rely on substances to cope with your sensitivity or not. Look at your feelings and ask yourself certain questions. The following questions will help you evaluate yourself to know whether you are addicted.

- Do I feel like overeating and drinking is the best way for me to cope with my sensitivity?
- Have I found it hard to stop overeating and drinking without my sensory overloads coming back?

- Am I sensitive to food?
- Do I engage in self-medication to deal with anxiety and stress I get from the world?

If your response to any of these questions is yes, you are in a swamp. You need to start making the necessary steps to deal with your addiction.

Start asking yourself questions on the following: How often you drink substances daily or weekly, and what is the quantity of the substances you take? How often do you overeat to deal with the feeling of overwhelming? Among the following: sex, shopping, gaming, gambling, love, the internet, which do you engage in to prevent yourself from anxiety and depression? Check yourself and identify any form of self-medication you may be into and start making plans to get yourself out of it. Nothing on the outside can make you feel fine and happy. It requires your effort. Happiness is more of a thing of the heart, not external. It's internal, and it requires internal inputs. You need to start loving yourself and caring for yourself more than others. Do not try to run from your sensitivities. Love yourself the way you are and make up your mind to stay away from any form of addictions.

HOW TO DEAL WITH YOUR ADDICTIONS

As empaths, you are endowed. You are a healer; hence, you need to work towards healing yourself of your illnesses and challenges. You can deal with your addictions. I have five ways for you to deal with your addictions and break loose so you can enjoy your life more.

- **Give Yourself Rest**

There are two different environments you can place yourself in. There is a kind of environment that will make you productive. It will demand your skills, and you will be able to function effectively. In a production environment, you are allowed to display your natural talent. This environment is usually where you find yourself as empathy daily when you help people with their emotions. In the environment, you are spending yourself. There is the second environment, which is the "reset environment." The reset environment is where you need to enter into once you have left the productive environment. Your activities in the production environment need to be replenished at the reset environment. Often, you find the reset environment in resting. When you fail to give yourself a sound rest, it will tell on your health. You need to know when to say STOP to yourself and rest so you can escape from an overwhelming environment.

- **Restore Your Energy From Time to Time**

Stop draining yourself without refueling. You need to be whole if you want to make others whole. Build integrity in your ability. Give yourself to the restoration of your energy and build your strength more. To restore your energy, you have to be connected to your source. Practice the methods listed in the previous chapters to stay attuned to your gift. The reason for your addiction is your vulnerability to negative energy and the overwhelming effects of draining yourself by helping others. When you restore your energy from time to time, you will be less vulnerable to overwhelming feelings, and there will be no need to take solace in any external substance.

- **Release Bad Energy**

You must make sure you do not give space for bad energy. You need to ask yourself this question: What am I holding on to? What emotions and feelings do I need to let go of? You may not be able to release all the bad energies at once; however, you can do it gradually. When you think you cannot do a thing or you cannot achieve a feat, the next result is usually to hold on to them. If you have pain in your heart that you have been holding on to, it is because you feel you cannot handle it. The feeling of unworthiness is the enemy you need to fight against. You can probably deal with the pain. You only need to look into yourself and find the healing power in you.

- **Manage Your Emotions, Time, and Energy**

When a person is not able to manage himself or herself, he or she ends up giving in to other means, such as addictions, which are not productive but affecting. You will often be tempted to think that your emotions are not weak; you don't have the energy or the time to deal with the overwhelming feelings you have. However, that is not reality. If you can manage your emotions, you will free some of the energy you spend on things that do not count. The best way to manage your emotions is to set boundaries for yourself. Know when to put all of yourself into a relationship and when to back out of the relationship. When you don't create boundaries, you will end up giving more of yourself, your time, and your energy, which will end up placing you in an overwhelming state.

- **Move and Avoid Isolation**

Aloneness is good for empaths, but loneliness is dangerous. Aloneness is different from loneliness. Aloneness is what you need to refresh your energy. It is therapeutic and saving. You do not go into aloneness and come back the same; there would have been certain changes. Loneliness, on the other hand, is an inhibiting state. It affects your productivity. It usually leads to isolation. When you are in isolation, you tend to move toward addiction. In loneliness, there is no liveliness, and it disrupts your mind. It can create a feeling of low self-esteem. It will seem like others are staying away from you intentionally.

Moreover, you need to be careful because aloneness can lead to loneliness. When you are stuck in your own time, and you fail to get out of it at the right time, you will end up feeling lonely. Move out by visiting your friends and having a good time with family members. Your dopamine will flow well when you engage in happy activities, which is what you can get by being with others.

Addiction is situated on the wings of both environmental and biological factors. As humans, we love to seek pleasure. Regardless of the source, whether it is from drugs, foods, rewards, games, etc., our brain activates the dopamine the same way for all activities we engage in that give us pleasure. To reiterate, every empath is prone to addictions because of their sensitivity to the feelings of others. They feel the fear, pain, anxiety, and even powerlessness of their society. When they are unable to process these feelings, they try to take refuge in external substances. You do not have to find solace in external substances; you only need to look into yourself. That is more than enough.

CONCLUSION

Empaths are natural gifts of God to humanity. They exist for our healing and edification in certain circumstances. One of the greatest gifts you can have as a person is to have an empath around you. Empaths are everywhere around us. You probably sat beside one on the bus while going to work this morning. The man next door might be an ideal representation of an empath. Having gone through the pages of this book, I hope you can now see empathy and recognize it. If you are an empath, I hope you have come to realize why you act the way you act, and you now know what steps you need to take to enjoy your life to the fullest. This book is a guide to make you a better empath if you are one and to make you have the best relationship with empaths that are around you if you are not. Just as the gold had to pass through the fire to become what it is, empaths, though born with their abilities naturally, undergo experiences to become what they are. If you have a child and you think you observe he or she is exhibiting one or more traits of the empaths listed in this book, you may need to pay attention in this chapter to have a glimpse of how empaths develop to become a warrior empath that can save others and retain his or her feelings. In this chapter, I will take you through the reasons people become empaths, and the stages they pass through to become empaths. Also, I will take you a little further into how you, as an ordinary person, can improve your empathy and be like empaths to help others.

THE REASON YOU ARE AN EMPATH

There are reasons for everything that exists. Empaths are born naturally; however, their talents become sharpened based on certain factors that surround them. Judith Orloff, the author of "The Empath's

Survival Guide," identified four reasons that make people become empaths. They are temperament, genetics, trauma, and supportive parenting. These four factors are crucial in making a person live his or her empath's life efficiently.

- **Inherent Temperament**

Every empath comes into the world with great power of sensitivity. Their sensitivity is beyond what is obtainable in this world. It is an inherent temperament. They show reactions that are more sensitive to what goes on around them, including light, touch, movement, smells, sound, and temperature. They are born with it as an instinct, and they cannot do away with it.

- **Genetics Transmission**

Genetics is also a factor that breeds empaths. Some of the sensitivities they possess can be genetically transmitted from their parents. Empaths can give birth to other empaths that will possess the same abilities they possess. Once a father who is an empath births another empath, it will soon become a family trait that moves from one generation to another.

- **Traumatic Experience**

When a child experiences abuse as a child, it can affect the way he or she sees the world. Trauma often affects the sensitivity of a child when he or she becomes an adult. When parents that are abusive train a child, depressed, narcissistic, or alcoholic, they usually have health challenges. They feel neglected by others as if the world does not care about them since it doesn't value sensitivity.

- **Supportive Parents**

With good parenting, it will become easier for a child to develop his or her gifts. Supportive parenting will help sensitive children to develop and hone their talents positively. They often mentor children, and they reflect their parents in the way they act. If you are already noticing the high sensitive rate of your child, you can be a contributing factor to how he or she will fare while using his or her ability to heal others.

THE EMPATHIC STAGES OF CHANGE

We all go through certain stages of transformation in our lives. It is part of living and development. The changes that occur at the different stages we encounter are determined by different factors, both external and internal. Empaths are also subjected to different stages in their personal development. I will call these stages "the empathic stages of change." These stages occur with their unique events. None of these stages is better. You only need to see the stages as the required period for real development into being a real empath. As you keep growing, you will experience the different events and experiences that are related to each of the stages. The stages are three, and they are the same for everyone; however, the journey the empaths take is different.

#Stage 1 – The Uneducated: Inclination toward others

The first stage every empath gets to is the stage where they are moved toward others and their feelings. At a young age, empaths look into other emotions and see their needs. They are sensitive to the world around them. This stage looks selfless, but it is an awkward stage for most empaths. The more emotions they are attached to, the more they feel they need to help those involved in those challenges. They always try to offer the help they can offer. At this stage, they begin to feel the pain of those that surround them, including their friends, family members, etc. Every moment of their lives at this stage is all about how they can help others solve their emotional problems. They often try every possible means to make others happy. They donate to others while they are still poor. At this stage, empaths are prone to the whims of narcissists and abusers. They do not have a full understanding of who they are at the stage. They often have challenges with their self-esteem, and they are always unsure of the future that lies ahead of them. At this stage, they are usually unintelligent.

#Stage 2 – The Seeking Stage: Inclination toward themselves

The challenges faced by an empath in the first stage will launch him or her into the second stage. The second stage is like a turnaround for the empath. He moves from being a savior to caring for himself only. He or she will stop giving himself or herself to others. The empath may end up standing against people they once cared for. At this stage, the empaths will try to stay away from the eyes of the world and be alone. They believe living alone will protect them from the challenges they faced at the first stage. They often spend this stage reflecting on themselves. They are involved in excessive growth processes, reading, meditating, and discovering their true self. At this stage, people will mostly consider them selfish.

#Stage 3 – Maturity: Inclination toward Everyone

The end of the second stage births a new experience for the empath. The empath will come back filled with experience, energy. The empaths will know his or her real self. The empath knows the limits, boundaries, and gifts he or she possesses. The empath has empowered himself or herself. The empath at this stage will be overflowing with love, and he or she is set to share it with others. Their joy in helping others is refueled, and they become more balanced, unlike their previous experience when they were drained by helping others. This stage shows maturity in their ability to use their gifts and their understanding of the gift they possess. The purpose of this book is to guide you to becoming a mature empath. You should know how to deal with others without losing your energy and draining yourself.

BECOMING AN EMPATH: EVERYONE CAN DO IT

Empaths have a special ability. Their ability is precedent on a general ability that all can learn, and that is empathy. The difference is that empaths are deeper in their expression of the empathy gift they possess. It is quite difficult, if not impossible, for anyone that is not born as an empath to express the gift of empaths. However, everyone can show empathy toward the other person. In this section, I will take you through how you can develop your empathy skills and understand people better. Practicing the tips in this section does not equate you to being an empath. However, you will increase the standard of your life by being empathetic.

If you can empathize with others, you will possess the following abilities.

- Ability to understand the needs of others
- Ability to resolve conflicts easily
- Ability to predict the actions of those around you and prepare ahead for them
- Ability to present your argument
- Ability to help people resolve some of their problems
- Access to people's trust
- Ability to decipher people's nonverbal cues

The abilities that you will have will aid your relationship with others and place you in the right position in life. To develop empathy, I have seven tips for you.

- Be a good listener when others speak to you. Your ability to listen actively will help you to identify their emotions and feelings.

- Create an image and see yourself as the other person. The visualization technique will work fine in this case. This requires you to think of what you would do if you were in that position.
- You need to deal with certain prejudices that may exist in you. Whatever beliefs you hold should not be held against everyone that you meet. Instead, you should deal with people on a global basis without any prejudice.
- Always focus on those things that connect you with the other person. Take your eyes away from your differences. The differences will affect the way you perceive them.
- To be empathetic, you need to show interest in people. Let them know you care about them. You can walk up to a stranger and ask questions of him or her. Expand your influence by being friendly.
- Deal with your mind. Make it know you care about someone or something. It all starts with the mind. Start building the thoughts of how much you care about a person, and in no time, you will live out those thoughts.
- Read fictional works. When you read fictional works, you will expose your brain to certain pathways that will aid your empathy. Fictional tales help you to replicate the happenings in the stories in the real world.

Everyone can express empathy. It is a gift that is present in humans: only that we express it differently. However, the empathetic ability can be enhanced by consciously paying attention to it.

Made in the USA
Las Vegas, NV
03 September 2023